	DATE DUE	

The Land and People of
ROMANIA

ROMANIA, a small country in southeastern Europe, has had a long struggle against division—not only the physical division of the land by the Transylvanian and Carpathian mountains, but the political and cultural separation among the Romanians, Hungarians, and Germans who live there. Romania's geographical position has made her susceptible to invasion and conquest, and she has also suffered in clashes between larger European nations; throughout Romanian history, sections of the country have been seized by—or awarded to—other powers.

In THE LAND AND PEOPLE OF ROMANIA, Julian Hale traces the history of the three principalities that now comprise Romania, and the slow process that led to unification and independence. He describes the present socialist regime, and the steps the Romanian people are taking to overcome the disadvantages imposed by Romania's geography and history.

PORTRAITS OF THE NATIONS SERIES

Also in the same format

The Land and People of
ROMANIA

by Julian Hale

PORTRAITS OF THE NATIONS SERIES

J. B. LIPPINCOTT COMPANY
Philadelphia   New York

U.S. Library of Congress Cataloging in Publication Data

Hale, Julian Anthony Stuart
  The land and people of Romania.

  (Portraits of the nations series)
  SUMMARY: Introduces the history, land, customs, industries, and people of
the Romanian Socialist Republic, the geographical intersection between East and
West.

  1. Romania—Juvenile literature. [1. Romania] I. Title.
  DR205.H3   914.98'03'3   78-151481
  ISBN-0-397-31288-1   ISBN-0-397-31188-5 (lib. bdg.)

Map by Donald T. Pitcher

Contents

Note

Most of the letters in Romanian words have the same sound as those in English words, but sometimes there are differences. In Romania, these are indicated by special marks above or below the letter in question. In this book, however, only two letters bear such differentiating marks, the letters ş and ţ. They are pronounced *sh* and *ts,* as in the *English sh*ow and ca*ts.*

The Land and People of
ROMANIA

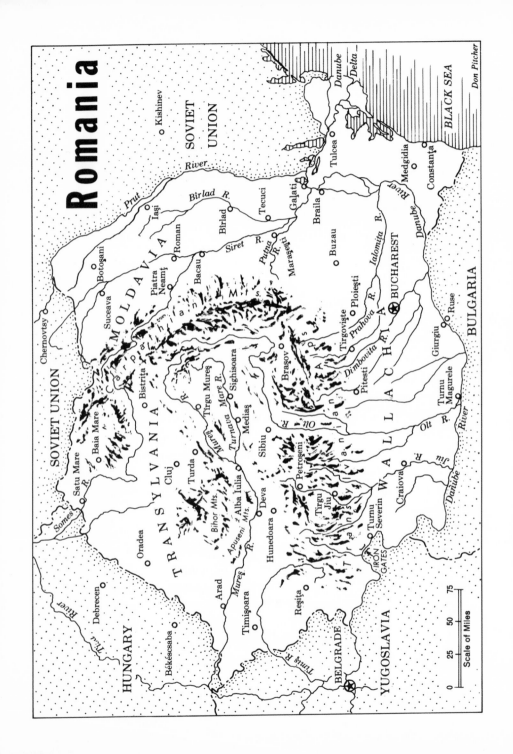

1

The Romanian Lands

Draw a line on a map from Baghdad to Berlin, and another from Paris to Samarkand. Where they cross, in the southeast corner of Europe, there lies Romania. Romania is an international crossroads —the intersection between East and West.

Across the heart of the country runs the curving line of the Carpathian Mountains. Westward lie the rolling hills of Transylvania, which descend into the plains of Hungary and Yugoslavia—then on to Austria and up again to the Alps and into Germany. To the east of the Carpathians stretch out the dusty plains of Wallachia and the green fields of Moldavia, which give way in their turn to the Black Sea and the vast Russian steppe. This same steppeland curves round to encircle Romania from the north; while, toward the south, beyond the slow waters of the Danube, Bulgaria separates Romania from Greece, Turkey, and the Orient.

Within these boundaries, and spreading out from the central Carpathian spine, lies the modern state of Romania. The Romanian Socialist Republic, as it is now called, is a country of 20,000,000 people. It is almost as large as the state of Oregon—and only just smaller than the United Kingdom. It extends up to 300 miles from north to south and 400 miles from east to west, and is bounded by a frontier only a fraction less than 2,000 miles long. Of Romania's

92,000 square miles, one-third consists of plains, another third of hills and plateaus, and another third of mountains.

Generally speaking, Romania, which lies exactly halfway between the North Pole and the Equator and next to the vast landmass of Russia, has long hot summers and long cold winters. Sometimes the temperature reaches well over 100° F. in the plains during the height of summer, and in winter temperatures as low as −37° have been recorded. However, these extremes, which come from the Russian heartlands, are usually met and softened by damp air from the west and mild Mediterranean air from the south. In the fall, when the northern forests are gold and crimson, some trees in the south seem undecided about the season, and fresh white blossoms push their way through the dead leaves on chestnut trees. But autumn always appears to be the shortest of the seasons; it is only a few weeks' wait from the last picnic on the beach to the first descent on the ski runs in the Carpathian resorts.

To most people who have not lived or traveled in this corner of southeast Europe, Romania is a remote and curious land. Even the people who do live there—descended for the most part from the original Dacian tribes and the Romans who first came as settlers and then as conquerors 2,000 years ago—feel a sense of isolation, surrounded by peoples of Slav and Magyar blood. But the "Daco-Romans" are proud of their Latin origins, of their Latin language and culture, and especially proud that they have survived centuries of bloodshed and oppression by invaders.

The Carpathian Mountains have always been the refuge of the native inhabitants in times of danger; they are the symbol of national unity. Though in one sense a barrier, they are also a rocky bridge between the Wallachian and Moldavian plains on one side and, on the other, the "land beyond the forest"—Transylvania. The Carpathian Mountains are a focal point of Romanian legend and folk-lore and a natural refuge. Four thousand feet up in these mountains

Statue of King Decebal of the Dacians, in Deva.

the Dacian king, Decebal, built his capital, Sarmizegethusa. You can still see traces of that ancient city; miles from any town or village, and very difficult to reach. Probably many other Dacian sites are yet to be discovered by archaeologists working in this wild and historic region.

A tradition of resistance clings to these mountains—peasants against feudal lords, Romanians against foreigners. The Carpathians are full of fortifications built over many centuries; they formed the main line of resistance to the invading Turks. Today these citadels, fortified churches and castles are merely tourist attractions, while the mountains themselves are a pleasure ground for climbers and skiers and artists. But if Romania were ever again invaded, the people would certainly make good use of their mountains to resist that invasion.

Rising in peaks up to 8,000 feet and more, the Carpathians are not quite high enough for the snow to last the whole year round. They sweep in a great arc from the wild Maramureş country in the north down to the Danube, where the river roars and tumbles through a narrow cleft in the towering cliffs—the Iron Gates. Today a massive dam and hydroelectric power station are taming these swirling, boulder-strewn waters, but traces of the bridge which Apollodorus of Damascus designed for the Roman invasion of Dacia in A.D. 106 still survive. So does an inscription marking the feat, carved into a slab of rock high above the torrent.

Beneath the high mountain peaks and across the Transylvanian hills grow great forests of spruce, fir, and pine, and mixed forests of conifers, oak, ash, and beech. Here the wolf and the bear, the chamois, lynx, and boar roam wild; and eagles, buzzards, and vultures hover and swoop overhead. In the many tiny lakes and streams swim thousands of trout, and high in the alpine regions grows the rare edelweiss, and the even rarer Piatra Craiului pink. The Apuşeni Mountains, an offshoot of the Carpathians, are studded with caves, and the rocks are twisted into strange and eerie shapes. It is the sort of country that brings the legend of Dracula back to life; indeed, the name Dracula, which means "devil," did belong to several of the more bloodthirsty princes of the dark ages. They were princes in name, but in fact little more than brigand chiefs.

Today, as always, Romania is above all an agricultural country. When the harvest fails, the country is poor; when conditions are kind and the grain and fruit are plentiful, the whole country is rich. This is in spite of energetic attempts by the present communist government to build up industries of all kinds, to provide a more uniform economy.

Though these new industries have brought many people off the land and into the towns, the majority of the Romanian population are still peasants. In spite of the introduction of some tractors and fertilizers, the methods they use to till the land are often little different from those their ancestors used centuries and centuries ago: the horse-drawn plow, the rickety wooden water mill. The villages are frequently no more than rows of wooden cottages along a main street, fronted by carved wooden gates and fences. The streets are dusty in the summer and deep in mud when rain has fallen. Around the villages stretch the fields of corn or sunflowers, wheat, fruit trees, or vineyards. In the mountains and around the villages of Transylvania, where the forests cover the landscape, piles of lumber fill the yards of thousands of local sawmills.

There is wealth, too, beneath Romania's soil. In Transylvania lie gold, silver, lead, and salt. Some of the salt mines, like the one at Ocna Dejului, in the heart of Transylvania, have been worked for nearly two thousand years. But this underground wealth never made the peasants who lived above it rich. The contrast between the gold beneath and the poverty above is still striking. The Moți people of the Apușeni Mountains have a saying, "There's gold in our mountains but we go begging from door to door."

Natural gas was discovered accidentally, it is said, by a shepherd in the middle of the eighteenth century, and scientists came from far and wide to study the extraordinary "inextinguishable fire" that had been set alight. But the gas wasn't exploited commercially until very recently.

The great variety of mineral waters below Romanian soil have been appreciated since Roman times. The baths at Herculane, for example, were discovered when Trajan's legionaries crossed the Danube into Dacia. Just as Romanians and visitors do today, these early colonists, nearly nineteen hundred years ago, used to drink the waters and bathe in them to cure a wide variety of ailments, from bronchitis to rheumatism.

Since those days, new wealth has been found in the form of coal and minerals such as uranium. Perhaps most important of all is the discovery below the southern Carpathian foothills of oil—the oil of the great Ploieşti fields, which look like Texas with a backdrop of mountains. This became such an important source of wealth that, during World War II, the Nazis regarded it as a major prize—and their occupation led in turn to the bombing of Ploieşti by United States planes. Today, oil is being produced in larger quantities than ever before. On the emblem in the center of the blue, yellow, and red Romanian flag is the picture of an oil derrick on a background of white mountains and green forests, surrounded by sheaves of wheat.

Another source of wealth in Romania is the Danube. This immense river is being improved for navigation and provides power at the point where it narrows down into the Iron Gates. The Danube is in many ways the lifeline of Romania. All Romania's rivers flow into this great waterway, which irrigates large tracts of land on either side of its banks. It is also a transport route, linking Romania with Hungary and western Europe and making prosperous ports out of the riverside towns of Galaţi and Braila. When the Iron Gates project is completed, and the system of dams and locks begins to operate, it will be possible to ship greater quantities of Romanian goods by this route than ever before. The raising of the water level has had one sad consequence. Downstream from the Iron Gates lies the small Turkish island of Ada Kaleh (which in Turkish means "the island fortress"). It is, or was, the only inhabited island in the Danube, with a mosque and a Turkish bazaar and a complete Turkish village. According to legend it was here, on Ada Kaleh, that the Argonauts returning to Greece found the olive and took it back to their own country. But now the island is no more, flooded by the rising waters of the Danube.

Before it reaches the Black Sea, the greatest river in Europe splits up into three broad channels and thousands of smaller canals, creeks, lakes, and backwaters. This delta covers 1,700 square miles—but only a few tongues of land remain *permanently* above water. Among these constantly shifting waterways grow tall reeds, which are converted into paper, fibers, and many other products. Often the reeds form whole islands of their own and float on the gently drifting currents.

The delta is a paradise for birds, including large flocks of pelicans, and in the water itself are vast numbers of fish. Out to sea, the sturgeon are netted and brought back to small villages at the edges of the delta and to places further down along the Black Sea coast, where their eggs, called caviar, are extracted for export all over the world.

Pouring its waters into the northernmost channel of the delta is the River Prut, which today forms the boundary between Romania and the Soviet Union. Beyond the Prut is the territory known as Bessarabia, after the Romanian Basarab family, and this land has been the object of dispute between Romania and Russia for centuries. Between 1918

Sightseers and fishermen on a small canal in the Danube delta.

and 1940, Bessarabia was part of Greater Romania, but today it forms the Moldavian Soviet Socialist Republic and the southern part of Bessarabia is included in the Ukraine. In other words, it all belongs to the Union of Soviet Socialist Republics. The River Prut is known popularly in Romania as the *riu blastemat*—the "accursed river"— because so often the Goths, Avars, Bulgars, Magyars, and many other invaders came across the Prut into the fertile Romanian lands, bringing with them pestilence and famine, killing the peaceful farmers they found in their way or driving them up into the mountains.

South of the Danube delta is Romania's one important seaport. Constanţa was built on the site of the ancient city of Tomis, which is a name well known to students of classical history. It was supposedly here that King Aetes of Colchis buried his young son who had been killed by Jason, leader of the Argonauts, after the capture of the golden fleece. Later, according to more reliable information, the Romans made the town into a large and prosperous port. It was to Tomis that the Emperor Augustus exiled the famous poet Ovid, who died there in A.D. 16. Today there is a statue to Ovid in Independence Square, on the site of the *agora* of Tomis.

A few miles farther north is the ancient Greek city of Histria, which was redeveloped by the Romans, after a period of stagnation when the port silted up. A number of cities were built on this site in the twelve centuries of its history, and the visitor today can see traces of them.

The region of the Black Sea coast is not only a museum of older cultures; it is also a treasure-house of ethnic backgrounds. Colonies of Turks, Russians, Armenians, Tatars, as well as Romanians and people of many other nationalities, live side by side all the way along the coast. And today the area is becoming even more international—at least during the summer tourist season. Since the early 1960s, tourists from all over Europe have come to resorts such as Mamaia to enjoy the warm sun and sandy beaches, and even, in some places, the health-giving qualities of the mud and the warm lakes. Mamaia looks almost

Modern hotels at Mamaia on the Black Sea coast.

like the Chicago lakefront, with tall glass-and-concrete hotels lining the brand-new promenades.

But visitors to Romania do not just come to lie on the sand of the Black Sea beaches. They come too to see the monasteries, particularly the ones with frescoes covering their inside and outside walls, which nestle in the folds of the hills in Moldavia and Bucovina, the northeast corner of the country. And they come too to see the towns. For, though still essentially an agricultural country, Romania's towns are growing fast and are taking on a new importance.

Already in Roman times, towns like Apulum (modern Alba Iulia, the home of Romanian nationalism in Transylvania) or Napoca (modern Cluj) were part of a network of flourishing trade centers in the outer provinces of the Roman Empire. Now there are ten cities with over 150,000 inhabitants. The biggest is the capital city, Bucharest, in the center of the Wallachian plains between the Carpathians and the Danube. To the Romans, Bucharest was just a small fortress on the banks of the River Dimbovița. Now it is a city of about a million and a half people, the administrative center of the country, and the center of many industries—especially machinery, chemicals, and textiles.

Cluj—Kolozsvar, in the Hungarian language of many of the people who live there—is the second biggest city and the main town of Transylvania. Its world-famous university is the result of a union of the Romanian and Hungarian universities. Cluj is the focal point for many Romanians of Hungarian origin. Until the end of the First World War in 1918, Transylvania belonged to Hungary within the Austro-Hungarian Empire. It was ceded to Romania at the same time as Bessarabia, in 1919, as a reward for Romania's entry into the war against the Germans: so "Greater Romania" came into existence only in the twentieth century.

Iaşi is the capital city of Moldavia. Frequently devastated during its turbulent history, is is now a home of the arts and of many new industries. We shall be seeing in more detail how the three main regions of Romania—Wallachia, Moldavia, and Transylvania—developed independently and then united to become the three most important elements of modern Romania.

2

A Time of Darkness and War

When the Roman legions crossed the Danube in A.D. 106, they met with stiff resistance from the Dacians. The "Dacii" were a proudly independent people of warriors and farmers. Scenes of their conquest are depicted on Trajan's Column in Rome. There is a monument in the Romanian town of Adamclisi, near the Black Sea, which also contains scenes of Trajan's victories over the people who lived to the east of the Dacian homeland.

The Dacians were defeated, but they were not destroyed. Before the Romans came, they were numerous and strong. Many years previously, they had been defeated by Alexander the Great, but their empire at its height stretched from present-day Czechoslovakia in the west to Bessarabia in the east and even south of the Danube into modern Bulgaria. Its heart, like the heart of Romania today, was the impregnable natural fortress of the Carpathian Mountains.

For the Romans, this northern outpost of their own huge empire was not at all an inhospitable land: they called it "Dacia Felix"—happy Dacia. The rugged Carpathians, after all, are cut through with pleasant, fertile valleys. What is more, the richness of the land to each side of the mountain range enabled the invaders to fill the granaries of Rome and still leave food to spare for the Dacians and the Roman colonists.

In the year 271, more than a century before the Romans began to abandon Britain, the Emperor Aurelian ordered their retreat from Dacia. The barbarians were closing in on every side. Some of the settlers stayed behind, but most left, and the territory that is now Romania was invaded and trampled for the next seven hundred years by wave after wave of tribesmen from the east, beginning with the Goths. Few of these invaders left traces which have survived in the Romanian lands. They pressed onward toward the richer prizes of Rome and Byzantium.

The Slavs, the Croats and the Serbs, the Bulgars and the Magyars: these were among the most powerful of the tribes that invaded southeast Europe and founded modern states there. But meanwhile nothing is heard of the Romanian nation, of the "Vlachs," to use the Slav word. No historical record of their existence throughout this dark age survives. Yet they must have existed, for they exist today and a whole nation cannot be created out of nothing. It seems as though the Dacians and those Roman settlers who stayed behind simply melted into the background. Probably they retreated into the Carpathian refuge and lay low, moving on whenever threatened.

Of course it was impossible to be isolated altogether. For instance, it appears that even before the seventh century the elements of Christianity had reached the Romanian people. Later, when the Bulgars held power in the region, they introduced to the Romanians the "Bulgaro-Slav" rite, which, centuries later, developed into the Orthodox Church. Again, the Romanian language during this period adopted many words of Slav origin, which indicates that the races did mix, even though the language remained basically Latin.

It is very unlikely that all the Romanian "Vlachs" were chased out of Dacia after 271. If they had retreated south of the Danube, as some historians suppose, there should be some record of their presence in what is now Serbia and Bulgaria. But there is no such record. Some Hungarians have wanted to prove that Transylvania, which corresponds to the central Dacian homeland, really belongs to them and them alone. They have claimed that not a single Romanian remained, and that their own ancestors, the Magyar tribesmen from the Asian steppes, took over a deserted land. The Hungarians have claimed that the Romanians returned there only in the thirteenth century.

No one can prove the case either way. The truth is as confused as the whole history of the dark ages, when hundreds of local chieftains were in constant conflict with each other, and the people of many different groups were fighting, then living peacefully with each other, then fighting again, and so on and on.

What is certain is that the Hungarian grip over Transylvania became stronger and stronger as the dark ages came to an end. In the year 1000 the Pope himself crowned King Stephen of Hungary. The Hungarian Empire flourished and expanded. Under Louis the Great, it extended south into Italy and north into Poland, although eastward its boundaries were limited by the tall range of Carpathian peaks.

The Romanian chieftains who lived in Transylvania became jealous of this new Hungarian power. Some of them crossed the Carpathians and set up their own states on the southern and eastern slopes and on the plains beyond. So it was that around 1300 to 1350 the two principalities of Wallachia and Moldavia were founded. After centuries of obscurity, we can now begin to trace the history of the states which were to become the cornerstones of modern Romania.

The founding of Wallachia and Moldavia did not mean that all the Romanians left Transylvania. A large population of Romanians stayed behind, only to become second- or even third-class citizens, remaining very poor and dominated by the all-powerful Hungarians. It is only in the twentieth century that Transylvania joins Wallachia and Moldavia, and all the Romanian people are united.

Compared to Western Europe, the new principalities were very backward. At the time of their founding in the early part of the fourteenth century, Dante was writing his *Divine Comedy* and England had its

Model Parliament. The early Wallachians and Moldavians lived in appalling conditions. The independence of their chieftains, who were little better than local brigands, did not bring prosperity. Imagine what it looked like in the principalities at this time. There were great expanses of empty countryside, with here and there little villages of mud and straw huts. The peasants dressed in the same homespun clothes they wore in Dacian times. They were probably even more ragged.

In the early days of Wallachia and Moldavia there were no towns of any note. Already some places along the trade routes to the Black Sea and the Danube were growing in importance. But the Romanians themselves took very little interest in trade and left that to the more capable hands of Jews and Greeks and Armenians, and even the Germans and Poles. The nobles, or "boyars," earned their fortunes like feudal landlords, living off their lands and paying no taxes. The Romanian peasants themselves scratched out a living from the soil, very poor, uneducated, guided by a rather primitive Orthodox religion.

Slowly, however, the power and the wealth of the princes grew, providing some protection against their unstable situation. The chief cause of their insecurity was the way in which they came to the throne. They were not born to it, on the hereditary principle, but were "elected" by the boyars. The assembly of boyars had the power to elect a new prince if the one already on the throne displeased them. But the prince had the power and the money to buy their loyalty. So, too, did any rich claimant to the throne.

There were endless feuds over succession because all members of the ruling family, as well as outsiders, were entitled to present their claims to the throne, in the absence of any laws of succession. As a result, the Wallachian and Moldavian princes followed each other with bewildering speed. After a short period of absolute power giving orders to his private council, squeezing taxes from the peasants, and ordering exotic punishments for anyone who displeased him, a prince would arouse jealousy, or make too many enemies, or be outbribed by a rival, and another would take his place.

Meanwhile, a new threat to these weak and erratic princely states was growing—the advance of the Turks. Throughout the fourteenth century, Bulgaria and Serbia, the states to the south of Wallachia and Moldavia, were being progressively weakened and broken up by the inroads of the Ottoman Turkish armies. In 1387, at the battle of Kosovo, the Serbs were defeated by the Turkish Sultan. Four years later, the Turks crossed the Danube for the first time ever and entered Wallachia.

At that time, Wallachia was ruled by an exceptionally strong prince, Mircea the Old. Mircea tried to enlist the support of the Hungarian kingdom against the Turks, and, although King Sigismund of Hungary organized a new crusade, all the knights of the West were unable to defeat the Turks. In 1417, Mircea was obliged to pay tribute to the Turkish Porte and, a year later, he died.

King Sigismund was still, rather fitfully, organizing resistance, using the services of the Wallachian princes who succeeded Mircea, such as Dan the Second and his younger brother Vlad, known as "Dracul" —the Devil. But Dracul (one of many chieftains whose name is the origin of the fictional Count Dracula) proved remarkably unreliable. In 1438, a year after Sigismund's death, we find the Wallachian prince invading his own homeland in alliance with the Turkish Sultan.

There followed a brief moment of respite, when a man named John Hunyadi, or John of Hunedoara, a Romanian by blood who had entered the ranks of the Hungarian nobility, drove back the Turks. But in 1444, as a result of treachery and misjudgment, Hunyadi was defeated at the battle of Varna, on the Black Sea coast, and there followed years of fighting, backward and forward, in Serbia, Bulgaria, and Wallachia, indeed in almost every part of the Balkan peninsula.

But the tide of history was in favor of the Turks. In 1453, they captured the Christian stronghold of Byzantium (Constantinople), and three years later Hunyadi died of the plague.

Nevertheless, the Turkish victory in the Romanian lands did not come immediately. In 1457, the statesmanlike Matthias Corvinus came to the throne of Hungary and made the line of the Danube solid against the Turks. However, on the throne of Wallachia at this time was a very different character indeed. He was the son of Vlad Dracul, and history knows him by the name of Vlad the Impaler. His greatest joy was to see his captives wriggling as they were stuck on high poles and left to die. Such tales of horror were told of him that even the Turks were overawed. But eventually the Turks drove the fearsome (and probably insane) "Impaler" out of Wallachia, and installed on the throne his more pliant brother, Radu the Handsome. From this point on, the resistance to the Turkish advance into the Romanian lands is left entirely to the princedom of Moldavia.

The story of the resistance put up by the Moldavians is very largely the story of their finest prince, Stephen the Great. Moldavia was isolated from the west—because the Hungarians, the Poles, and the Russians were all preoccupied with their own struggles; and from the south —because the Turks dominated the Danube approaches. Stephen's only defense was his army of Moldavian peasants and a burning belief in the need to protect Christianity from the infidel Turk. His first act was to capture the port of Chilia, now only of military importance, because the Black Sea trade route had been cut by the Turks. But two years later, in 1467, the Hungarians, under Matthias Corvinus, suspected the Moldavians of treachery and attacked them from behind. Stephen cunningly led the Hungarian soldiers on into his own territory and fell on them in the night. Corvinus escaped, wounded, and Moldavia was free to face the Turks once more.

Sure enough, the Turkish attack came. And again, using the same tactic of evacuating the population and food before the advancing

Stephen the Great, Prince of Moldavia.

army and then making a sudden counterattack, Stephen inflicted a crushing defeat on the Grand Vizier Suleiman the Eunuch, his pashas, and his troops. But the Turks had an almost endless supply of soldiers, and soon they were back in Moldavia again. Stephen, harassed by a simultaneous attack from the Tatars in the north, was temporarily defeated, but rallied with Hungarian support and made the Turks retreat. This victory gave Moldavia several years of peace.

Before Stephen died in 1504, after forty-seven years on the throne of Moldavia, he built up a name not only as a soldier, but as an administrator and a patron of the arts. In particular Stephen is remembered for founding a number of remarkably beautiful churches and monasteries, many of which stand today.

The construction of the monastery at Putna began in 1466, after the dimensions had been decided in the traditional way—that is, by selecting the place where the main gate was to be built, and firing an arrow; where it landed was the exact spot where the altar of the central church should be placed. Although the monastery has been devastated many times in its history, it still stands, in its reconstructed form, on the original site—nestling, like almost all the great Romanian monasteries, in a fold in the forested hills at the head of a valley. In its treasury you can still see some of the fifteenth-century embroideries, chalices, and rare manuscripts from this thriving center of early Moldavian culture.

Another remarkable construction of Stephen's is the monastery church of Voroneţ. Its main charm is the frescoes, added in 1547, covering all the walls of the church, inside and out. One of the motives for painting the walls in this fashion was certainly to encourage the people in their struggle against the Turks: at Voroneţ, you can still see, in the pure natural colors of the time, a picture of the Day of Judgment, where the damned are unmistakably Turkish (Tatars also). Similarly, at the nearby church of Moldoviţa, there is a scene in the frescoes of the siege of Constantinople, where the Christians are shown gallantly resisting the Turks. All this was a sort of early propaganda, an encouragement to the morale of the army of poor peasants, which was all the Moldavian princes could raise, and a promise to them of eternal salvation for taking part in the holy war.

Unfortunately, however, the princes themselves were rarely of the character of Stephen the Great. His own son, known as Bogdan the One-Eyed, was typically weak, grasping, and treacherous. On the throne of Wallachia, too, were a whole succession of men who were ever prepared to betray their countrymen to the Turk in return for personal favors or money. One of the most treacherous, yet curiously effective in his resistance of the Turks, was an illegitimate son of Stephen the Great, Peter Rareş, who also became Prince of Moldavia. But even he could not stop the slow but sure process whereby the

Turks and Christians battling at Constantinople, from a sixteenth-century fresco at Moldoviţa, Moldavia.

princedoms of both Wallachia and Moldavia were forced to submit to the Sultan. It became the practice for the princes to buy their "election" to the throne from the Turks, who manipulated the corrupt and self-seeking claimants. These claimants were not all Romanian by any means. Any adventurer who would or could pay more than his rivals into the Porte's treasure chest became the prince. One prince of Moldavia, who reigned for two years before he was betrayed and killed, was a Greek called Jacob Basilic, at one time a convert to the Protestant religion, and also a mercenary in Spain and Italy, who made preposterous claims to imperial Roman descent.

During this whole period of three centuries from the foundation of Wallachia and Moldavia, the pattern of life for the Romanians living across the Carpathians in Transylvania hardly changed at all. The territory of Transylvania was frequently involved in the wars between the Turks and the western European powers, as we have already seen.

But for the Romanians the most important thing that happened was the consolidation of Hungarian power. They were affected more by social changes than by political or military events. In Transylvania the population was becoming divided more and more rigorously into two separate groups. On the one hand, there were the privileged peoples: the so-called Received Nations. These were the Magyars; the Szeklers (also Hungarian by origin, but a distinct group of early settlers); and the Germans (or Saxons, who, like the Szeklers, had been encouraged to colonize Transylvania and defend the outlying areas of the Hungarian kingdom). These people monopolized political power. The mass of Romanians, on the other hand, had no power and no rights at all. Already, as we saw, some had fled Transylvania because they were oppressed and had founded Wallachia and Moldavia. Those who remained behind were treated more and more as third-class citizens. They were poor and ignored by those of Hungarian and German blood.

Not all the Hungarians and Germans, however, could benefit from their acceptability as members of the Received Nations. Despite the growth of towns in Transylvania at this time, most of the people, like the Romanians, were poor peasants. They all suffered together the devastations of the seemingly endless wars with the Turks. On occasion they rose together against the feudal overlords, but the result was only more bloodshed during the inevitable reprisals which followed. The first great peasant uprising took place in 1437 and was only crushed after more than a year.

In 1514, there was a vicious peasant war which was bloodily repressed. The peasant leader was put to death, in the western Transylvanian town of Timişoara, in a particularly cruel fashion. He was made to sit on a throne of red-hot iron and a red-hot crown was put on his head to mock his pretensions. His body was then torn to pieces and hung up in several of the large towns. So many of his followers were killed, that the Hungarian army was for many years deprived of its contingents of Transylvanian peasants, both Magyar and Romanian. This was one reason behind the victory of the Turks in the decisive battle at Mohacs in 1526.

As a result of this battle the Turks gained control of the entire kingdom of Hungary. In 1541, Transylvania became a separate principality—under Turkish suzerainty. This meant that the Transylvanians had to pay an annual tribute to the Porte, hand over their trade to the Turks, send soldiers to the Turkish army, and do nothing which conflicted with Turkish interests. Theoretically, as in Wallachia and Moldavia, the princes were elected by the nobles, but in practice it was the decision of the Turkish Sultan that counted.

This, then, was the situation at the end of the sixteenth century. But in the year 1600 something occurred that pointed the way forward more than three centuries to the time when the Romanian lands were finally united. In that year, if only briefly, Wallachia, Moldavia, and Transylvania were united under the leadership of one man, Michael the Brave. It is not quite such a heroic story as it may sound, for Michael had the treacherous nature of all the princes of the time. Nevertheless, by a long series of bargains, battles, beheadings, and murders, and by siding with the Magyar nobles in Transylvania at the expense of the peasants who shared his Romanian origin, and by a military conquest of Moldavia, he did succeed in bringing the princedoms together under his own rule.

But then King Rudolf of Hungary, suspicious of Michael's motives, plotted a revolt by the Magyar nobles. After a series of intrigues, forged letters, and rapidly changing loyalties, Michael the Brave was murdered on the orders of a Hungarian general. The brief flicker of Romanian unity was snuffed out.

3

Wallachia and Bucharest

Once Michael the Brave had left the scene, all three principalities relapsed into a situation not far short of anarchy. But in Wallachia, in 1632, a prince by the name of Matthew Basarab came to the throne and remained there for the unusually long period of twenty-two years. He was remarkably clever at playing off the interests of the three foreign powers that had designs on Wallachia—that is to say Turkey, to whom Matthew had to pay personal homage, Hungary, and Russia. He also carried on a constant feud with the prince of Moldavia, Basil the Wolf, who was jealous of Matthew's prestige.

During Matthew's reign, cultural life in Wallachia began to develop, in particular the publication of religious books. It is also the time when Greek influence was first felt. At the court of the Turkish Sultan, many of the most important functions began to be taken over by men of Greek origin. Since most came from the Phanar, or "Lighthouse," quarter of Istanbul, they were known as the Phanariots.

In 1679, one of these rich and influential Phanariots, who had settled in Wallachia, decided that he would buy the princely throne for himself. It cost him a fortune, but he managed to stay on the throne for the next ten years. During his reign, the first Romanian Bible was printed, known as "Şerban's Bible" after the prince, Şerban Cantacuzene.

All during this period, the last half of the seventeenth century, we see a revival of the aggressive ambitions of the Turks. Since one key factor in their plans was to attack Hungary, this frequently involved the participation of the Wallachians. The Sultan's army would pass through Wallachia on its march westward, and would demand that the prince on the throne of Wallachia—since he was a vassal of the Sultan—should provide food and soldiers for the campaign. In 1659, the Turks insisted that the capital of Wallachia should be moved from Tirgovişte, in the Carpathian foothills, to Bucharest, on the Danubian plain. They knew that they could keep better control over the principality if its seat of government was far away from the traditional refuge of the Carpathians.

In 1683, Prince Şerban Cantacuzene was forced by the Turks to be present at the historic siege of Vienna (so too was the prince of Moldavia). This was the turning point in the fortunes of the Turks. Had they captured Vienna they might possibly have advanced into the heartlands of western Europe, and the whole course of European history would have changed dramatically. But Vienna stood firm. The Hapsburg empire was saved, helped by that great Polish patriot, John Sobieski. Şerban Cantacuzene had brought 4,000 men to serve in the Turkish army outside the city walls, yet he too played a part in the victory of the Christians. He sent secret information about the Turkish army to the defenders in the city and, according to one unreliable report, substituted balls of straw in place of cannon balls. When the Turks retreated, he left behind an unmistakable sign of his sympathies with the Christian defenders. He erected a cross where his soldiers had been with a Latin inscription hailing it as the symbol of the true church which is the conservation of the world.

The relief of Vienna soon led to the retreat of the Turks from Hungary too. The Hapsburg Emperor Leopold, in Vienna, even had ambitions to drive the Turks as far back as the southernmost borders of Wallachia. But it came to nothing.

Palace of Mogosoaia, near Bucharest, built by the Brincoveanu family.

Meanwhile Constantin Brincoveanu succeeded to the Wallachian throne, and he spent the twenty-six years of his reign desperately playing off one power against the other in an attempt—a successful attempt as it turned out—to keep some measure of independence for his principality. His methods were bribery, trickery, and cultivating influence at the Sultan's court. It was very difficult to do otherwise. The Turkish rule was so strong, and their methods so cruel, that the princes were reduced to using any means they could to keep at least a small measure of freedom. They believed that the ends justified the means. (In the same way, subsequent rulers of Romania have always had to combat the superior force of foreign oppressors. Today, that oppressor is the Soviet Union rather than Turkey; but the lessons learned from the princes' struggle against the Sultans have served the modern rulers in good stead.)

The peace of Karlowitz, in 1699, was an important landmark. The big powers agreed that Transylvania should come under Hungarian control and that Moldavia should be freed from Polish pressure; but Wallachia was left in the same precarious situation as before. In order to ease the burden of the Turkish impositions on Wallachia, Constantin Brincoveanu appealed to the Russian tsar for help. He allied himself with a distant cousin on the Moldavian throne, Dimitrie Cantemir, and waited for the Russian troops to advance. This they did, but were speedily repulsed by the Turks, leaving both Wallachia and Moldavia to their fates. Brincoveanu was betrayed by all his colleagues and delivered into the hands of the Turkish envoy who had come to seize him. The old man was then taken to Istanbul, thrown into prison, and tortured in front of his children, who were then beheaded, together with Brincoveanu himself, in a ceremony attended personally by the Sultan.

At the beginning of the eighteenth century, the Greek Phanariot influence was really taking hold in Wallachia and Moldavia. The Turkish Empire was in decline, and the Austrians captured and held Wallachia for several years, up to 1739. However, the Turks rallied, drove out the Austrians and, in an attempt to stop the riot, the Sultan decided to put men who were completely dependent on the Porte on the thrones of the Romanian principalities.

But these Greek princes proved no more reliable or efficient than their Romanian predecessors. In the next hundred years, up to 1821, when the Phanariot rulers were overthrown, the average length of a prince's reign on either throne was two and a half years. The princely title was constantly changing hands, and one man might regain the throne several times during his lifetime, and, on different occasions, rule over both Wallachia and Moldavia.

The princes had power of life and death over their own subjects, but were on the other hand slaves of the Sultan. They could, and did, devise hideous punishments for those who displeased them, and they demanded that anyone coming to see them should kiss the hems of their clothes. But, in the presence of the Sultan, the prince had to perform exactly the same humiliating ceremonies himself. The princes dressed in furs and flowing Turkish-style robes, which the local boyars copied, without ever daring, however, to dress as lavishly as their masters. But the vast mass of the people, the poor peasants, lived in miserable huts like animals, and frequently starved. Because the prince was forced to pay the Sultan vast sums, first to buy the throne and then to keep his position, he was constantly thinking up new tricks to extract money from the people.

Picture the Wallachian court around 1700. (It would not have been very different in 1500 or 1600, nor was it to change except in details during the following century of Phanariot rule.) The princely palace was the most imposing building in Bucharest, but that is not saying much. The walls were plain, with windows constructed high up, just under the wooden roof, to prevent enraged citizens from climbing in. The decorations on the outside were sparse, only a few Turkish-style twisted columns beside the windows and doors. The prince lived more like a rich merchant than the ruler of a country. He would personally hear petitions and cases at regular Divans, while reclining on an Eastern couch (hence the English word "divan"). In the palace court-yard merchants and peasants and officials crowded each other, shout-ing and crying. Animals found their way into every corner. The women were shut away in a secluded part of the palace. According to some accounts, other rooms were full of the prince's jewels and other valuables—furs, icons, money, and so on—packed in chests, ready for rapid removal should the political situation require instant flight.

While in power, the prince underlined his superior position by de-manding the humiliation of others, including the boyars. Under Turk-ish influence, they adopted the habit of moving around the palace supported beneath the shoulders by high officials. Few boyars were allowed to sit in the prince's presence.

Travelers from the west were not frequent at this time, although some individuals, like the Reverend Edmund Chishull, an Englishman, did record the experiences of their voyages to and from Turkey. Chis-hull, in 1747, wrote of his experiences in Wallachia: "The lands of the province are entirely in the hands of the Prince and barons; the rest are rustics, being all either slaves or servants. . . . The power and act of pronouncing sentence is wholly in the Prince, after which, as commonly in Turkey, the execution immediately ensues." He had this to say of the capital city: "Bucharest is a large straggling town of a very peculiar make, the outward parts very mean, consisting of houses, the greater part of which is underground like our cellars, and covered over at the top with straw or bark of trees."

The population of Bucharest seems to vary with the accounts of different travelers, but was probably at this time in the region of 60,000. More than other European towns in the eighteenth century, Bucharest was dirty and smelly. By the beginning of the nineteenth century, however, some efforts were being made to improve its appearance, with more attention paid to the rows of wooden planks that served for roads in the city center. Nevertheless, to this day, Bucharest does seem to be a huge village as much as a capital city, with peasants' cottages and their hen runs lining the back streets in straggly lines. In very recent years many of these poorer areas have been cleared for the construction of modern apartment buildings.

Traveling in the Wallachia of two centuries ago, and up to quite recently too, was a dangerous affair. William Wilkinson, the British consul in Bucharest at the beginning of the nineteenth century, wrote of a typical journey in the countryside: "A kind of vehicle is given, which is not unlike a very small crate for earthenware, fastened to four small wheels, by the means of wooden pegs, and altogether not higher than a common wheel-barrow. . . . Four horses are tied to it by cords, which form the whole harness; and, driven by one postilion on horseback, they set off at full speed, and neither stop nor slacken their pace, until they reach the next post-house."

As for the natural wealth of Wallachia, most was taken away by the Turks. Almost no goods beyond the bare minimum, and hardly any of the money collected as taxes, remained in the principality. The peasants found themselves obliged by new laws to work harder and longer, for no gain to themselves. But, in all the Romanian lands, this period also saw the slow growth of manufacturing industries.

Only rarely was there a ruler in the principalities who was wise and farseeing enough to reform the worst abuses. Such a man was Constantin Mavrocordato, who, in the course of several reigns, succeeded in righting some of the worst wrongs, stopping the emigration of the peasants, and reducing some of the taxes. However, the Sultan disapproved even of these reforms and deposed and imprisoned Mavrocordato. His reforms were at once reversed.

In the early 1770s, after the army of the Empress Catherine the Great defeated the Turks, both Wallachia and Moldavia came for four years under Russian control. Not for the first—or last—time, the principalities were used as pawns in vast diplomatic maneuvers. On this occasion, Austria, Hungary, and Russia were dividing up the powerful state of Poland. The principalities were quite simply items in the bargaining of the big powers, until by a treaty in 1774 the Russians handed them back to the Porte. The only gain to the Romanian people were some concessions concerning the freedom of the Christians to practice their religion there.

Russian influence was strengthened at the expense of Turkey a few years later, when a Russian consul was appointed at Bucharest. The appointments too of Austrian, French, and British consuls only rubbed in the fact of the decline of Turkish control.

Meanwhile, the despotic rule of the princes continued. Prince Alexander Ypsilanti, in his eight years on the Wallachian throne from 1774 to 1782, introduced a new code of justice, founded badly needed schools, and eased the burden of taxation on the peasants. But he was, it hardly needs saying, an exception. Soon another war broke out between the Turks on one side, and the Russians and the Austrians on the other, and the Romanian lands were once more the scene of the fighting.

In 1791, a group of boyars made an appeal to Austria and Russia for the creation of a separate Wallachian nation. They asked to be allowed to be neutral in the quarrels of the Great Powers. Of course the appeal went unanswered, but it does represent one of the first signs of national pride and a desire for independence. It also shows that, even in isolated Wallachia, the ideas of the French Revolution were in the air, although they did not affect the particularly corrupt princes at the end of the eighteenth and beginning of the nineteenth century.

A new Russian-Turkish war in the early years of the nineteenth century saw a Russian administration in Wallachia under the clever but dissolute Russian commander, Kutuzov. But, after negotiations involving not only Russia and Turkey but also Britain and Napoleon's France, control over the principality was yet again returned to the Turks in a treaty in 1812. In this same Treaty of Bucharest, control over that part of Moldavia known as Bessarabia, in other words the eastern part lying between the rivers Prut and Dniester, was given to Russia. (And Russia kept control until the revolution at the end of World War I. It is for this reason that, in 1940, Soviet Russia laid claim to Bessarabia, and, after victory in World War II, has retained it ever since.)

In 1821 a new movement burst on the scene, first in Moldavia and then in Wallachia: a revolt in the name of Greek freedom, led by Alexander Ypsilanti, grandson of the Wallachian prince of the same name. But before Ypsilanti and his "brigands," as the boyars called them, could reach Bucharest, the situation was further complicated by another popular revolt—this time in the name of the *Romanian* people. This movement, led by a Romanian of peasant origin called Tudor Vladimirescu, was hostile to the Greek influence in the Romanian lands, and even attracted some support from the minor Romanian boyars. But Vladimirescu was murdered by one of Ypsilanti's henchmen, and his movement collapsed. Then Ypsilanti was himself defeated by the Turks and fled to Transylvania. But his uprising did signal the start of the revolution in Greece, a revolution that caught the imagination of the Western world, and in which the great English poet, Lord Byron, met his death.

Nor, in the end, was Vladimirescu's movement a failure. For in 1821 the Turks decided to end the system of Phanariot rule. From this moment on the princes on the thrones of Wallachia and Moldavia were Romanian, though they still had to maintain a delicate balancing act between the Turks and the Russians.

The Turkish Empire was now so weakened by internal quarrels (and massacres) that Russian influence soon began to dominate. In 1828, a new Russo-Turkish war broke out and, inevitably, the first Russian move was to occupy the principalities. However, there were some advantages in the Russian rather than the Turkish presence: independence in their own affairs was given to the Romanian princes and boyars, and the levies to the Turks were finally abolished.

Once peace was signed, the Russian governor, Count Kiselev, introduced a relatively enlightened system of laws, and a new constitution, which, being the same for both Wallachia and Moldavia, made things easier when, thirty years later, the two principalities united. Kiselev is still remembered in the name of a wide tree-lined boulevard which is the main route from the north into modern Bucharest—in Romanian *Şosea Kisseleff*.

In the 1840s there were definite signs of a movement among the boyars and the people for a union of the two principalities. In 1846, the customs barriers between the two were abolished.

But the real move toward unity occurred in 1848, a year when the whole of Europe was in a state of revolution. Many of the boyars, as well as the Russians, were hostile to any form or idea of liberalism, such as the spread of education or the right of the ordinary people to be at least consulted in decisions which affected them directly. But others had been influenced by a French education and were developing a pride in the Romanian people; in other words, they were becoming what we now call nationalists.

The nationalist movement was stronger in Wallachia than in Moldavia. In 1848, a revolutionary committe of Wallachians was formed in Paris, and then came to Bucharest. The prince was evicted. Under such men as Ion and Dimitrie Bratianu, C. A. Rosetti, and Nicolae Golescu, a revolutionary government, with representation by both peasants and boyars, was formed. But it was only short-lived, for the Russian army intervened. Russia had not been affected by the 1848 ferment and was determined to crush its effects wherever she could. Russia was (and still is) an eastern power, suspicious of the dangerously liberal ideas of the west. The Romanian lands were (and still are) so close to Russia that this eastern influence is not difficult to impose whenever Russia thinks it necessary.

So between 1848 and 1851 a Russian army was once again in occupation of Wallachia and Moldavia. Anyone who took part in the 1848 revolution was banished. Yet the prince of Wallachia, Barbu Ştirbei, continued with a program of reducing the impositions on the peasants such as compulsory road building, of making the landlords pay a small share of the taxes, and of giving an education to more and more people. Ştirbei also began to organize a Wallachian army and frontier guards. Wallachia was, in other words, just beginning to look like a modern, independent state, at least on the surface.

In 1853, however, the Russian army was back again in the principalities. The tsar, by now old and given to mysticism, believed that the moment had come to establish Russian control over them once and for all at the expense of the Turks, and to protect forever the Orthodox Christians from the infidel. He wanted the princes to break off all relations with their "suzerain," the Sultan. The Turks resented this highhandedness; so too did the Romanians, who saw it as a maneuver merely designed to increase Russian power. Finally the western powers objected strongly. When the tsar's army invaded the principalities, they united against Russia, and this was one of the causes of the Crimean War. As a result of the more general conflict, in which Russia was dangerously isolated, her army retreated from Wallachia and Moldavia. But the principalities were not destined to be left in peace yet. Instead the Austrian army followed the retreating Russians and occupied in their turn the whole of Wallachia and Moldavia.

The situation of the principalities caught between the intriguing great European powers as well as Russia and Turkey now gets more complicated than ever. In 1855, the French suggested that perhaps the best solution for Wallachia and Moldavia would be as one single state under the same prince. But that idea was dropped largely at England's insistence (for England believed in supporting Turkey for her own interests). Austria all along considered that she had secured control over the principalities forever by virtue of her military occupation.

By now a few Romanians were beginning to see that perhaps the confusion of the Great Powers might be used to the advantage of the Romanian people. In Paris an important group of exiles, including many names from the 1848 revolution, were busy putting forward the claims of *one* Romania, including Transylvania in their grand design.

They played a notable part in persuading the French Emperor, Napoleon the Third, to support their cause. Eventually, in 1856, with the signing of the Treaty of Paris, it was generally agreed that no power was to enjoy "exclusive protection" of the principalities. The road was now open, after centuries of foreign aggression, occupation by Turks, Russians, and Austrians, and complicated international diplomacy, for union and independence.

But for the moment, let's go back again in time and see in a little more detail the development of Moldavia and its capital Iaşi, as the more northerly of the two principalities moves gradually toward union with its southern neighbor, Wallachia. And then we shall see how union was finally achieved.

4

Moldavia, Iași, and Union

Because they were neighbors, because their populations were Romanian, and because both were for a long time under Turkish rule, Moldavia and Wallachia had many of the same experiences even in the early period of their history.

Lying to the north of Wallachia, Moldavia was plagued not only by Turks and Russians. Up until the partition of Poland in 1772, Moldavia also had to contend with Polish armies invading her territory in support of their claim to its ownership. The Tatars, too, frequently descended out of the vast Russian steppeland and attacked the Moldavians, burning the towns and villages and stealing the crops. This was the constant background to life in Moldavia in the early years of its history.

Basil the Wolf was the first prince on the Moldavian throne after the brief spell of unity under Michael the Brave. He is mainly remembered for his jealousy of the Wallachian prince, Matthew Basarab, whom he tried to unseat. But during his reign, cultural life in Moldavia did develop; for instance, in 1646, Basil's Code of Laws was printed at Iași, the Moldavian capital, at a printing house which the prince himself had founded. This, it is claimed, was the first code of laws ever to be published in a national language in Europe. The press was established in the monastery of the Three Hierarchs, and the church of this monastery, built under Basil's direction in 1638, still stands. Its walls are covered by intricate stone carving, which was originally gilded; but the gold melted when the monastery was set on fire in later years.

The city of Iași became the capital of Moldavia in 1565, when it was already a well-established town, known particularly for its trade. By the middle of the eighteenth century, there were probably about 30,000 people living there. Like Bucharest, Iași was mostly composed of rough huts, with muddy or dusty tracks connecting them, and even the prince's palace was not a very impressive building. The countryside was frequently flooded and communication difficult. But both in Iași

Seventeenth-century church of the monastery at Dragomirna.

and in the many monasteries which sprang up all over the principality, some men were able to escape the rigorous life of the time and devote themselves to the arts.

An especially violent time occurred in Moldavia after the Turkish retreat from Vienna—a time when, in Wallachia, Constantin Brincoveanu was maneuvering cleverly to keep the peace. Poles, Russians, Cossacks, and Tatars all invaded the principality. It was not until the Peace of Karlowitz in 1699 that the Poles agreed to evacuate Moldavian territory.

Moldavia was next involved, indirectly, in the war between Peter the Great of Russia and Charles the Twelfth of Sweden. After Charles's defeat at Poltava in 1709, the Swedish King and his Cossack ally, Mazeppa, retreated to Moldavia and lived for five years in the town of Bender, which as a result came to be nicknamed Carlopolis.

Then there came to the throne of Moldavia a remarkable man, Dimitrie Cantemir. He was at first appointed by the Turks; the Sultan trusted him to seize the prince of Wallachia, Constantin Brincoveanu, who was causing them so much trouble. But far from carrying out the Sultan's will, Cantemir negotiated with Brincoveanu, as well as with the Russians, whom he saw as the force of the future in the Balkans. Promising Cantemir a hereditary crown for his help, the tsar ordered an attack on the Turks, but, as we saw in the previous chapter, the Russians had underestimated their enemy and Moldavia was abandoned to its fate. Cantemir escaped and fled to Russia, hidden in the rugs of a princely carriage, and became a notable figure in the Academy of Sciences at St. Petersburg. He was elected later to the Berlin Academy, as a pioneer of historical research. He was one of the very first to develop the thesis of the Latin origins of the Romanian people. Indeed, it was only this time that the term "Romania" began to be used in academic circles.

During the Phanariot period that now followed, in Moldavia as in Wallachia, there were few princes of note. Nicholas Mavrocordato, who had three terms on the Moldavian throne at the beginning of the eighteenth century, did go so far as to consult with the boyars before making some decisions, but on the whole the princes behaved like the most extreme despots. The only possible excuse for their brutality is that they were constantly exposed to danger, both to their own person and to their country.

Such a time of danger was during one of the many Russo-Turkish wars in the late 1760s and early 1770s. At the end of the war, negotiations for the partition of Poland were in full swing. The Great Powers greedily demanded any portion of Europe that they felt they could gain at the bargaining table. For Moldavia the result was that, in 1775, the northern part of the principality, known as Bucovina, was given by the Porte to the Austrians. Bucovina remained in Austrian hands until the collapse of the Austro-Hungarian Empire in 1918. In addition, this was the time of growing Russian control over both the principalities. It was less than forty years later, in 1812, that Moldavia was further dismembered by the Russian annexation of Bessarabia.

More and more, Moldavia and Wallachia were beginning to be seen as one unit by Romanians and foreign powers. But those who held the power in the principalities had as yet no interest in formal unity, being too jealous of their own privileges. Besides, the Turks preferred to keep the two apart in order to control them more easily—the age-old principle of "divide and rule."

Ever since he became prince of Moldavia in 1819, Mihai Sutu supported the movement for Greek freedom, which was championed by Alexander Ypsilanti. When Ypsilanti and his men first reached Iaşi in the spring of 1821, their banner was blessed at the Church of the Three Hierarchs by the Metropolitan, the chief of the Orthodox Church in Moldavia. But when the Greek cause appeared to be lost, Sutu submitted to the demands of the Russians and of the Moldavian boyars and relinquished his throne. It was left to the Wallachians, under the leadership of Tudor Vladimirescu, to try and profit from the unrest in order to raise the banner of Romanian freedom. The peasantry in Moldavia were even more downtrodden than in the slightly richer lands of Wallachia, and they had neither the resources nor the energy to revolt.

After the Russian commander, Kiselev, had left the principalities in 1834, the throne of Moldavia was occupied by Mihai Sturdza, who remained there for the next fifteen years. He was responsible for a number of reforms: building roads and bridges, establishing hospitals, a postal service, schools, and the first faculties of the University of Iaşi.

It was here in Iaşi that Mihai Kogalniceanu began to lecture in Romanian history, proclaiming the unity of all the Romanians and anticipating the 1848 revolution and the movement toward the union of the principalities. This led in 1843 to the suppressing of the Iaşi Academy at Russian insistence. But the ideas themselves could not be suppressed. Four years after the "revolution" of 1848 (which was in Iaşi scarcely a revolution at all), the writings of Kogalniceanu were

Church of the Three Hierarchs in Iasi.

again published in Moldavia. It was now only a matter of time and favorable circumstances before union of the principalities was achieved.

At first circumstances were distinctly unfavorable. As we saw in the last chapter, the Russian army, closely followed by the Austrian army, marched into Moldavia. The whole project of union had to wait until the Great Powers could work out the fate of the principalities. They had to agree on a solution with the Turks, because, it must not be forgotten, both Moldavia and Wallachia were still under the suzerainty of the Sultan.

The idea of union, as the first step toward complete freedom and independence, was gaining ground all the time. Napoleon the Third of France was the most ardent champion of this cause. In Moldavia the French consul intrigued against the Austrians and the English, both of whom opposed the union. The French also fought to overcome the opposition of the man whom the Turks had just appointed to rule Moldavia, Nicholas Vogorides. Vogorides, a Greek whose loyalty was entirely with the Sultan, spoke scarcely any Romanian.

Despite opposition from the French, Turks, Vogorides and so on, more and more intellectuals, boyars, and peasants in Wallachia and Moldavia came out in support of union. Moldavia, the smaller and weaker of the two, had more to lose by union, since Bucharest was bound to become the capital city. The issue was put to the vote in July 1857. The unionists lost, but there was so much blatant cheating by the antiunionists (the English, still anxious to support the Sultan, were largely responsible for this) that the French insisted the election should be annulled and a new one held. In Britain, the following year, the injustice was partly redressed by Gladstone, who spoke in favor of the Romanian right to union.

New elections were held in the principalities, and this time the result reflected Romanian opinion fairly: there was a strong majority in favor of union. It was agreed by all that a foreign prince should be chosen to rule the united country, so that neither Wallachia nor Moldavia should be specially favored. Mihai Kogalniceanu spoke eloquently in the Moldavian Divan, or council, pleading for five points: autonomy (that is, self-government), union, a foreign prince, government by representatives of the people, and finally neutrality. These were accepted by a huge majority. The same enthusiasm for this program was found in Wallachia.

The Great Powers haggled over the whole problem, until, in August 1858, it was agreed that the Romanian provinces were now to be *called* the "United Principalities of Moldavia and Wallachia," but they would still be under the suzerainty of the Sultan, and they should have *two* princes and *two* governments. A Central Commission was set up to work out new laws that were the same in each principality, and all class privileges were formally abolished. But the peasant was not given the vote; for that privilege a man required a sizable income.

Still there was not complete union. The unionists therefore hit upon an ingenious plan to achieve their aim: get the same prince elected in both Wallachia and Moldavia.

That was easier said than done. At the elections in Iaşi in December 1858, the unionists did not fare very well against the boyars who were intriguing for their own candidates to the throne, and the result was deadlock. But then a compromise candidate came on the scene, a man called Alexander Cuza, who had been appointed as commander of the Moldavian troops. Suddenly, all parties agreed, and Colonel Cuza was elected prince of Moldavia.

Meanwhile, in Wallachia the elections were just beginning. Again, no one could find one candidate who had the support of the majority. The conservatives and antiunionists were the most powerful group, but they could not agree among themselves on a candidate. The unionists all the time were arousing public support for their cause, and when the name of Alexander Cuza was put forward, the Wallachian Assembly acclaimed him as their prince too.

In spite of the maneuvers and negotiations of the Great Powers, the

Romanians had achieved on their own the union of Wallachia and Moldavia.

Alexander Cuza was not a particularly noteworthy, or noble, personality. He had dabbled in politics on the side of the Liberals in the 1848 movement and been exiled. He was made prefect of Galaţi, a port on the Danube river, by the Greek prince Vogorides; but he soon rejected his sponsor. He himself said that he doubted if he was fit for the job of ruling over the United Principalities. But from the very beginning of his reign, he was helped by French diplomatic and military support. Cuza was also fortunate to be left in peace by the Austrians, who at the time were preoccupied with the independence of Italy.

Finally the Great Powers recognized the fact of union, and this was confirmed in 1861 by the Sultan himself. In February 1862, the two assemblies joined together as one in Bucharest.

During the first years of his reign, Cuza had to carry on a running battle with the conservative politicians especially over the question of land reform. The Conservatives were mainly from the boyar class, big landlords who had no interest in seeing more land given to the peasants. Also there was the quarrel with the monasteries, which sent a large part of their wealth abroad to their "protectors" in Jerusalem, Athos, and other Orthodox Holy Places. By the middle of the nineteenth century, these monasteries, founded by Romanian princes and boyars, owned almost a third of all the land in Moldavia and a quarter in Wallachia. It was obvious that the Romanians needed to keep the income from these vast estates in their own country. Eventually, when the Greek monks refused to accept any offer of compensation from Cuza's government, their properties were taken over without compensation. This angered the Conservatives.

In 1864, Cuza made a direct appeal to the peasants, who, in a hurriedly organized vote, gave him absolute power to do whatever he wished. In return for the peasants' confidence, Cuza passed a sweeping Agrarian Law, which freed them from all their ties to the landlords, abolished slavery, and gave them land. But the results of these good intentions were not altogether good; for in many cases the plots which the peasants received were too small to be cultivated economically. Nevertheless, the law was a big change from the past. So too was the law which set up new schools and universities and laid down the principle of free education for all.

In spite of these excellent blueprints for social reform, Cuza's personal life was becoming a public scandal. It was even rumored that he was trying to secure the succession to the throne for one of his mistress's sons. He was deserted by some of his best advisers, such as Mihai Kogalniceanu, and finally, after a riot was brutally suppressed in Bucharest, the Conservatives and the Liberals both agreed to remove Cuza from his position as dictator. On the night of February 23, 1866, the conspirators burst in on Cuza, who was in the palace with his mistress. They made him sign his name to a note announcing his resignation, the paper supported by the back of a Romanian officer. He was at once escorted out of Bucharest, and then across the frontier. The next morning the population read notices in the streets proclaiming that a foreign prince was to be elected to govern them, as the unionists had always intended.

Behind the scenes, furious diplomatic maneuvers were going on to find a prince who would be acceptable to the Romanians and to the Great Powers—and who also was prepared to take on the job. Finally, a man was found—Prince Charles of Hohenzollern, a man of both German and French royal descent. In a vote in the principalities, he got the approval of the people, although there were some in Moldavia who were beginning to wonder if they wouldn't be better off separate from Wallachia. Prince Charles himself was hesitating, because he foresaw Russian as well as Turkish opposition to the whole scheme, and he also hesitated to become the Sultan's vassal. But, following the advice of the great Prussian premier, Bismarck, he eventually took the plunge.

The only problem that remained was: How to get to Romania? It obviously was not possible to go by sea via Istanbul, nor via Russia. Prussia was about to go to war with Austria at any moment. This meant that, for a Prussian officer and prince, the risk of going openly by the most direct route through Austria was too great.

So, with a false Swiss passport, the prince boarded a train bound for Odessa on the Russian Black Sea coast. He traveled in goggles to disguise himself. He had to sit in an unusually (for him) uncomfortable second-class carriage. On one occasion, he was very nearly recognized by some Austrian officers he had once known. He then changed to a Danube steamer, and was joined by the Romanian who had been responsible for his appointment, Ion Bratianu. The two men pretended not to know each other. As soon as the steamer touched Romanian soil, at a town called Turnu Severin, the prince was bundled off the boat, his haste making the captain thoroughly suspicious. But it was too late for anyone to prevent the prince's landing in his new country. After a two-day drive across the Wallachian plain, Prince Charles of Hohenzollern reached Bucharest on May 22, 1866—in a torrential rainstorm.

5

Transylvania and Cluj

Transylvania, the "land beyond the forest," is a romantic name. It suits the countryside with its rolling hills, fertile valleys, and the craggy line of the Carpathian Mountains. But life in Transylvania in the Middle Ages was not romantic, except for a few who were rich and well born. Sometimes the tensions boiled over. In 1437 and again in 1514 there were terrible peasant revolts. There was also unrest over religious restrictions. Although Roman Catholics and Protestants were allowed to worship freely, the Romanians—who were Orthodox Christians of the eastern Byzantine rite—were not allowed the same freedom. This was so in spite of the fact that there were more Orthodox worshipers in Transylvania than Calvinists, Lutherans, or Roman Catholics.

In 1600, as we saw, Michael the Brave ruled briefly over Transylvania, as well as over Wallachia and Moldavia. But the Hungarian, Szekler, and Saxon nobles, who took back the power afterward, were doubly determined that the Romanians in Transylvania should never again get to such a position. All contact between Transylvania and Wallachia was forbidden. Orthodox priests were made especially unwelcome: a visiting Metropolitan from Wallachia was once given a public whipping. The Romanian population was deprived of any rights at all as citizens of Transylvania.

But Transylvania did have some independence as a state at the be-

Transylvanian wooden church in the Maramureș region.

ginning of the seventeenth century, when the Hapsburg rulers of Austria and Hungary were struggling with the Turks for control over the whole of this part of south and central Europe. The princes of Transylvania managed to keep a balance between the two great rivals and to spend their time improving the standard of life in their province. But this was the time of the Thirty Years War in Europe so they also had to reckon with a further source of strife: the counterreformation, the struggle by the Roman Catholics to regain their hold over people who had turned to the Protestant faith. Gabriel Bethlen (or Bethlen Gabor), prince of Transylvania between 1613 and 1629, played an important role in keeping Transylvania both independent and basically Protestant.

The princes who succeeded Bethlen came from the Rakoczy family. In the early 1660s, George Rakoczy the Second found himself involved in a major war between Hungary and the Turks over his own Transylvanian territory. This long and terrible war, which had its climax in the siege of Vienna in 1683, marks the end of a golden age in Translyvania.

Just as the defeat of the Turks at the gates of Vienna was a turning point in the fortunes of Wallachia and Moldavia, so too did it change the situation in Transylvania. Although the Turks tried a counterattack into the province in 1691, Transylvania was confirmed now as a self-governing state, legally united with Hungary, but responsible in the last resort to the Austrian emperor. It was rather a complicated compromise. The result was that for a long time Transylvania was in many ways a free and independent state—though ruled, one must not forget, by the *three* accepted peoples (Magyars—that is, Hungarians—Szeklers, and Saxons) and not at all by the mass of the Romanian people.

There was one way in which the influence of Austria was felt: that was in the burning question of religion. The court in Vienna was strongly Roman Catholic, and a scheme was thought up there to undermine the Protestant control of Transylvania. The idea was to get the downtrodden Orthodox priests and as many of their Romanian flock as possible to unite with the Roman Catholics. The device used was a new, "Uniate," church combining the Greek and Roman rites. In a decree of 1699, the so-called "Uniates"—those who joined this new combination—were declared to enjoy the same rights as Catholics in Transylvania. This angered the Calvinists particularly, because they had hoped to drive as many Romanians as possible to *their* religion. Instead, many Romanians decided to become Uniates, seeing all the advantages, material and political, that it would give them.

A brief attempt by the Transylvanian prince Francis Rakoczy to extend his rule to other parts of the Austrian Empire failed. In 1711, Austrian domination over all Hungary, and therefore over Transylvania, was confirmed. There began a long period of relative calm. The Diet, or Transylvanian parliament, met and made decisions, but all along it was the final decision from the Austrian capital of Vienna that really counted.

In the eighteenth century, the Hungarians and the Saxons (Germans) began to quarrel more and more openly. The Saxons were richer than the Hungarians or the Szeklers (and far richer, of course, than the Romanians), which made the others envious. Besides, the Magyar nobles felt that they should have the same privileges in Transylvania as their fellows had in Hungary proper—including the privilege of avoiding taxes.

In the last part of the century, the Austrian emperor, Joseph the Second, visited Transylvania twice. As a result, he abolished the old constitution and ordered a new one, which followed more closely the Hungarian system. However, this was not at all popular in Transylvania. Both the Magyars and the Saxons felt that they were worse off than before. The Magyars began to press more and more for a complete union between Transylvania and Hungary. In this way they hoped that both the Saxons in Transylvania and the Austrian emperor would have less influence over what they saw as their own Hungarian affairs.

As for the Romanians, they continued to live their miserable lives. The old laws which deprived them of all rights and privileges were still applied. Some were extremely humiliating: for instance, it was decreed under the laws of 1540, laws which lasted into the eighteenth century, not only that no Romanian was allowed to hold any official position, but also that no Romanian was allowed to wear boots or shoes, only sandals, and that no Romanian was allowed to live in a house which had a window looking out on the street. This is why, in Romanian villages, you still see all the houses built sideways to the road.

But the Romanians did have some champions. One was a man called Ioan Inocenţiu Micu (or Klein, to give him his German name), who was appointed to supervise the Romanians in Transylvania. In 1733 he was made a member of the Diet. He made such a fuss about the miserable condition, first of the Romanian priests and then of the whole Romanian people, that the Austrian emperor appointed a commission to investigate. The Magyars and the Saxons were furious, and Klein was publicly abused. They replied to his claims in a pompous and high-handed way. "The Uniate Bishop and clergy," they wrote, "demand things which no-one has ever demanded from our ancestors and could not demand from our descendants, things in the highest degree contrary to the ancient privileges and exemptions acquired from our kings and princes . . . in short, things which it would never be fitting should belong to the Wallach clergy and plebs, in view of their well-known character." It is obvious that the Romanians were not likely to get very far faced with this sort of opposition. But Klein kept up his campaign nevertheless. Eventually he was obliged to flee to Rome and made an appeal to the Pope. But that came to nothing, and Klein, now desperately poor, stayed on in Rome as an exile until his death. He left behind in Transylvania such a ferment among the Romanian peasants that one day their rights as citizens would have to be respected.

It was inevitable that this religious and social persecution should lead in the end to violence. But still the Magyars and the Saxons refused to include even the Uniate, still less the Orthodox, Church among the "Received Religions" of Transylvania.

There was unrest too among the Magyar and Saxon peasants. Even though they were not oppressed for their race, as the Romanians were, they were still regarded as hardly human by the nobles. When the Emperor Joseph the Second came to Transylvania, first in 1773, and again in 1783, he received thousands and thousands of petitions from peasants of all races. This made a deep impression on him. The visit also impressed the peasants, and there are many in Romania today who can describe in great detail the visit of the emperor, as the story was handed down from their great-great-grandfathers.

Joseph's reforms—though they were quite mild and only directed against some of the most extreme abuses—had an electrifying effect. In October 1784, the peasants felt confident enough to fight the nobles. Three men came to the front as leaders: Horia—who had somehow or other managed to get a personal interview with the Emperor Joseph —Cloșca, and Crișan. Horia believed that the emperor supported a peasant uprising, and soon the whole revolt got out of hand. Castles and nobles' houses were burned down, and the peasants went on the rampage. That was something the emperor decidedly did not support. The revolt was bloodily repressed, and, although the peasants were granted an amnesty, a cruel punishment was reserved for the three leaders. Crișan escaped by committing suicide, but Horia and Cloșca were taken out to a big field, where thousands of people gathered to watch, and broken on the wheel; then, while still alive, disemboweled. Their limbs were then cut up and sent around the country as an example.

Horia, Cloșca, and Crișan.

The place where they were executed, just outside the town of Alba Iulia, is still called Horia's Field.

The emperor did not approve of the cruelty of these punishments. The consequence was that more reforms were instituted by which the Romanians were recognized as citizens and the peasants freed from slavery. But it was not long before the old feudal ways were restored, and Joseph died a deeply disappointed man.

Yet the Romanian struggle went on. An appeal was made once again to the Transylvanian Diet and to the Austrian emperor (now Leopold the Second) for equal rights for the Romanian nation. The Romanians claimed they were the oldest people in Transylvania; and this marked the beginning of the never-ending historical argument over the mysterious "disappearance" of the Romanians after the Romans had left Dacia. The appeal was rejected outright in the Diet, needless to say. But meanwhile Romanian national feeling was growing stronger. It was boosted by a visit to Rome made by some young men studying to enter the Romanian Church. They saw there, depicted on Trajan's column, the scenes of the resistance of the Dacians to the Romans. This was a spur for the study of the origins of the Romanian people, and also for the study of the Romanian language. The idea of the return of ancient Dacia (that is modern Transylvania) to the Romanian people was in the air.

It was not to happen for a long time yet. There now began a period of reaction by the Magyars which lasted all through the nineteenth century and into the twentieth.

One of the most important ways in which the Magyar nobles dominated the other ethnic groups was to make the Hungarian language the only official one. Anyone in an official position, in government, in the churches (of all faiths), in the schools, in all the professions, had to be able to speak and write Hungarian. Hungarian, by the way, is a very difficult language as it has nothing in common with other European languages, with the one exception of Finnish. Of course, the

Saxons resisted this—as did the Romanians—although the latter had no voice in the Diet.

The process of Magyarization continued inexorably on all fronts. One of the reasons why the capital of Transylvania was transferred in 1790 from Sibiu to Cluj (where it has since remained) was that Cluj was basically Magyar, while Sibiu was Saxon. Cluj had for long been a prosperous place. Indeed, under the name of Napoca, it was known as an important town in Dacian times. Later it became the center for the Hungarian military domination of Transylvania, and developed in much the same way as many of the provincial towns under Austro-Hungarian influence.

In the Diet, held now in Cluj, the Hungarian nationalists put forward their program to make the Magyar influence dominant in the province. Not all Magyars were extreme in their views, however, and there were lively debates among them as to the policy they should follow. But there was a general tendency by all the different national groups in the Austrian Empire (for example the Croats and the Slovaks) to want to govern themselves as a nation. Clearly the movement for the union of a Magyar-dominated Transylvania with Hungary was gaining the upper hand. The movement was first led by Baron Wesselenyi, then joined, and gradually taken over by, the extreme patriot, Louis Kossuth.

Then came the 1848 revolution, which swept across Europe like a forest fire, engulfing many countries, including Hungary. Kossuth's revolutionary views, as well as his championing of the union of Transylvania with Hungary, carried the day.

The Saxons and the Romanians protested—loudly. In a field outside the small town of Blaj, known since as the Field of Liberty, about 40,000 Romanians met in a vast protest meeting. They protested both against union with Hungary and against the denial to them of all rights as citizens.

Their appeal did not go unheard by the authorities in the Hungarian capital, Budapest, nor by such men as Baron Wesselenyi in Transylvania. A law was drafted to guarantee at least some Romanian rights, including the use of their language. But Hungary's situation was becoming desperate as the Austrians fought back against the breakup of their empire. The fiery uncompromising Kossuth once again dominated the Diet with his eloquence, with the result that the law guaranteeing Romanian rights was never passed.

A civil—or rather racial—war now broke out in Transylvania, with the Magyars fighting the Saxons and the Romanians. Atrocities were committed on both sides. But Kossuth was also waging war against the Austrians. Even the Russians, who were then installed in Wallachia and Moldavia, became involved against him. In fact Kossuth made almost every non-Magyar the enemy of the Magyars. It was too much. The Hungarian national revolution was crushed. The Austrian reaction was almost as cruel as the deeds done in the war.

The defeat of Kossuth accomplished little for the Romanian people. There followed a period of Austrian rule which repressed all the minority nations in the empire. But then Austria became involved in a wider war—in the west—and the situation in Transylvania looked as though it was going to go back to what it had been before 1848.

There was first, however, a brief period of Romanian and Saxon victory. In 1863, the Transylvanian Diet was called, not in the Magyar town of Cluj but in the Saxon town of Sibiu. There was a clash of views between the Magyars and the Austrians, and the upshot was that the only delegates at the Diet were Saxons and Romanians. They passed laws at once which gave the Romanian nation, churches, and language equal status with those of other nationalities. Of course the Magyars regarded these laws as invalid. It was not long before the situation was back to "normal," and Hungarian control over Transylvania was reestablished. In 1867, Austria and Hungary adopted a formal constitution which gave them more or less equal rights as partners in a joint Austro-Hungarian Empire. Transylvania came under the direct control of the Hungarian capital, Budapest. Once again the Romanians were not even consulted. They were now a small minority in the Kingdom of Hungary, no longer the majority in the province of Transylvania.

The first line of resistance for the Romanians was the church. They were lucky in having at this period a remarkable man as the Orthodox archbishop, Andreiu Şaguna, who, in a calm, statesmanlike way, built up the church as the focal point of Romanian national life.

All the time Magyar attitudes were hardening against the Saxons as much as against the Romanians. The Magyars believed that the best solution was to turn the whole population into Magyars, speaking Hungarian as their mother tongue. In spite of formal laws which guaranteed tolerance of ethnic differences, other laws were made which had quite the opposite purpose. Worst of all, no notice was taken of those laws which protected the Saxons and the Romanians. For example, the Romanian language was almost never heard in the classrooms of high schools or in the courthouses. In the Parliament in Budapest, Romanian deputies were often shouted down with cries of "Go back to Bucharest." The Romanian press was persecuted and censored. The result was that, for years on end, the Romanians merely adopted a rather hopeless policy of passive resistance. This also meant that they did nothing to become "Magyars." They refused to take Hungarian names, and Romanian (that is to say, Latin) names became very popular in the last half of the nineteenth century. People began calling their children Ovid, Virgil, or Trajan, Octavia or Lucretia, names that could not be put into Magyar, because no Magyar version of them existed.

In 1881, a Romanian National Party was formed, but it achieved nothing. Any protest against the Magyar regime was punished. In 1890, the party made a first appeal to the outside world for help. Ties with the United Kingdom of Wallachia and Moldavia grew stronger.

In 1894, there was a spectacular trial of a group of Romanians who had attempted to petition the Austrian emperor. Since the trial was held in a Magyar court in Cluj, the result was of course heavy prison sentences to all concerned. The Romanian National Party was thereby forcibly dissolved. But the world now knew much more about the plight of the Romanians in Transylvania.

During the rule of Baron Banffy in Budapest, from 1895 to 1899, more and more oppressive methods were used—not only against the minorities, but also against the Magyar workers and peasants. Many poor Hungarians protested by rioting or by emigrating, often to the United States. In the early part of the twentieth century, the government in Hungary was in a continual state of crisis. What is more, Hungary's partner in the empire, Austria, was becoming very disturbed with the Magyar excesses, because they threatened to upset the stability of the empire. Franz Joseph, the Austrian emperor, was even more worried by the prospect of social change if the opposition in Hungary was in power. Only his son, Franz Ferdinand, showed signs of sympathy for the non-Magyars. Meanwhile the persecution of all the non-Magyars in Hungary (including Transylvania) continued.

The elections of 1910 in Hungary were a real battlefield. Repression of the poorer classes and of the Romanians, Serbs, and other non-Magyars under Hungarian rule was rampant. Over two million people left Hungary between 1900 and the outbreak of World War I in 1914.

Events in the whole continent of Europe were now building up to a dangerous climax. The Balkan wars (as we shall see in the next chapter) showed just how near total war was. The Great Powers were maneuvering with each other to further their national interests. There was mistrust everywhere. Soon world-shattering events were to put the problem of Transylvania into the background.

On June 28, 1914, in the town of Sarajevo, in the state of Bosnia, the son of the Austrian emperor was murdered. Franz Ferdinand was gunned down by a Serbian terrorist. The reasons for the murder are confusing enough, but the effect was immediate. It led to the outbreak of World War I. It was this war that changed the fortunes of all the Romanian lands—Transylvania as well as the already united Wallachia and Moldavia.

6

The Struggle for Freedom

We left the united principalities of Wallachia and Moldavia just at the moment when the German Prince Charles of Hohenzollern had arrived in Bucharest, after his secret journey across Europe. That was in the early summer of 1866.

The Turks, who still were the suzerains of the new principality, protested strongly. They were only just restrained by the European powers from attacking across the Danube.

In July 1866, a new constitution was drawn up and passed by the Romanian Parliament. It was a liberal constitution, guaranteeing basic rights to all citizens; but it sounded a good deal better than it was in practice. The old habits of corruption and arbitrary rule did not die away overnight, but the constitution was far more liberal than anything that existed over the border in Transylvania.

Above all, it was sound enough to survive with only minor changes until 1918, when the principalities—or, as we can now properly say, "Romania"—united with Transylvania.

The union of all the Romanian people was not by any means possible back in the time when Prince Charles came to the throne. It was in the next year, 1867, that the arrangement was made to create a joint Austro-Hungarian Empire, putting Transylvania—including all the Romanians there—under Hungarian control. We have already seen how tight that Magyar control was.

The first priority now for the united principalities of Wallachia and Moldavia was to rid themselves of Turkish suzerainty. To start with, Turkish recognition of the prince was obtained, though reluctantly. Nothing final could be done until the Romanian army was thoroughly reorganized. When Charles became prince, discipline was very bad and the military equipment old and insufficient. The new prince, with the directness of a true Prussian, set about building the army up again. He also was a frequent visitor to the European capitals, trying to get diplomatic support for Romania, and, incidentally, finding for himself a wife. The woman he chose, a German princess, became famous in Romania in later years for her literary talents and her charitable works, and was known affectionately as Carmen Sylva.

Meanwhile the political situation inside Romania was far from stable. Prince Charles himself was not an absolute ruler like the princes of the past. At first there was little he could do, other than watch as governments fell, to be quickly replaced in elections that were in every case corrupt and illegal. At the same time, the prince had to endure many insults because of his Prussian origin, since popular feeling in Romania was much more sympathetic to the French. This was the time, too, of the famous war between France and Prussia (1870), when Paris was besieged and battered by the Prussian guns. Prince Charles was also criticized for giving the contract for an important state railway to an exceedingly unreliable Prussian Jew—a scandal which came to involve the entire Prussian state. The prince was saved only by a rally of the conservative forces inside Romania and an election which was even more rigged than the previous one.

So Charles managed to hold onto his Romanian throne, but Europe as a whole was still in a dangerous state. In 1876, Serbia declared war on the Porte in an attempt to free herself from Turkish control. A war between Turkey and Russia (which supported Serbia) was likely at

The Romanians attack at Smirdan in the war of liberation against the Turks. Painting by Nicolae Grigorescu.

any time, especially as Serbia had miscalculated Turkey's strength and was being overrun.

As so often in history, the Romanians seemed doomed to become involved in any war between the Slavs and the Turks. And sure enough, after a great deal of international bargaining and secret agreements, war did break out. The Romanian government voted to support the Russians and not the Turks, and in the spring of 1877, the Russian army advanced. Simultaneously, the Romanians declared themselves free forever of Turkish suzerainty. This time they were not to be disappointed. The Turks were never to return. They had been in Wallachia more or less permanently since 1391, when they first crossed to the north bank of the Danube. Now at last their day was over, after almost five hundred years.

But freedom was not won just at the stroke of a pen. Freedom had first to be won by arms.

To start with, the Romanian army was not involved in the fighting between the Russians and the Turks. But when the Russians were pinned down just south of the Danube, near a place called Plevna, Prince Charles brought across a large Romanian army to help them. At once he was offered the command of all the operations against the Turks. This meant that both he and Romania were now completely committed to the struggle. The result of the hard fighting that followed was total success, and the Romanian soldiers were hailed as heroes.

Romania at last was free of the Turks—but not now of the Russians. Though allies against the common enemy (that is, the Turks), they did not agree about the peace that followed. The main reason for this was that Russia wished to annex the southern part of Bessarabia—the easternmost part of Moldavia—in spite of the fact that her claims to this territory were quite unsound. Russia had seized most of Bessarabia in 1812 with equal lack of justification. The tsar of Russia saw this corner of Romanian territory as the rightful spoils of victory, even if an ally had to provide those spoils. It was the price that Romania had to pay for Russian help in gaining her own independence. The European powers cared little about the whole matter, and Romania was not even a party at the Treaty of Berlin which settled it.

Although Romania was now an independent state, recognition was refused by the European powers right up until 1880 because of quite another problem. That problem was the treatment of the Jews in Romania.

The majority of Jews who lived in Romania in the second half of the nineteenth century were quite recent arrivals in the country. In the Moldavian capital of Iaşi, about half the poulation was Jewish. The Jews, however, had never been allowed to become citizens of the country. They were obliged to remain apart from the Romanians in other ways. They could not buy land or even become innkeepers. In the 1866 constitution, drawn up when Prince Charles came to the

Romanian throne, one article specifically forbade Jews from holding the rights and privileges of Romanian citizens. So the Great Powers declared that they would not recognize Romania until that article was taken out of the constitution.

The Romanian government, especially the Conservatives, who were also frequently landlords and who owed money to the Jews, were frightened that if all the Jews were to become Romanian, they themselves might simply be bought out. Romanian business, such as it was, was indeed dominated by the Jews, since few Romanians had the skill or the energy to make a success of a commercial or industrial career.

Debates raged in the Romanian parliament. But the European powers insisted that the law should be changed. There were many anti-Jewish demonstrations in Romania, and the publicity they received in western Europe made the governments there even more insistent. Finally a new law was passed, which made some, but not the most important, concessions to the Jews in Romania. The Great Powers were satisfied. Even Bismarck, the German chancellor, withdrew his opposition, though this was largely because he was offered a settlement on the thorny question of the Romanian state railway.

Then, on May 22, 1881, the newly accepted state of Romania became a kingdom, and in the cathedral of Bucharest, Prince Charles of Hohenzollern was solemnly declared King Carol I. His crown was made of metal from one of the Turkish guns captured at the battle of Plevna.

Soon afterward the veteran politician, Ion Bratianu, the same man who had guided the new prince secretly into Romania, became once again the prime minister and ruled for the next seven years with almost dictatorial powers. There began a period of industrial expansion, although this did not involve any profound social changes. It was still very much a question of middle-class and boyar domination. Even the so-called Liberals were in favor of strong rule by the rich and the well-born. The king became a large landowner, by far the largest in the country, and he was learning now how to use effectively his ultimate control over the government, with his powers to dismiss and appoint ministers.

It was King Carol's influence that was at least partly responsible for Romania's seeking her international security by siding with the "Central Powers," that is to say, Austria-Hungary and Germany. In spite of a growing feeling in Romania that *all* Romanians should be united (including those in Hungarian-controlled Transylvania), such an alliance seemed to him the best course. Neither the king, nor indeed the Romanian government, saw much hope in the alternative—a useful and long-lasting alliance with Russia (especially after the seizure of Bessarabia). And France was hopelessly weak. So in 1883 a secret treaty between Romania and the Central Powers was signed. It was *so* secret that not even the Romanian parliament knew about it—only the king, Ion Bratianu (the prime minister), and Dimitrie Sturdza (the foreign minister). Amazingly enough, in the years to come, when other ministers came to power, it was King Carol *alone* who knew of this vitally important treaty. He kept the only copy in a private safe in his mountain castle.

In 1893, Prince Ferdinand, the king's nephew and the appointed heir to the Romanian throne, married a granddaughter of Britain's Queen Victoria and the niece of the former Prussian emperor. This strengthened the international ties of Romania with the great European powers.

Inside Romania the situation was not so stable. For one thing, the peasants were becoming more and more impatient with their mistreatment by landlords, many of whom were absentee landlords. From time to time, the government in power attempted some land reforms, but the results were never satisfactory. Speculators would take advantage of any new law which put more land up for sale, and the peasants were worse off than before. There were frequent riots against the big landowners' property. A very small-scale workers' movement also began in the last years of the nineteenth century.

Nor were the governments themselves stable. There was a constant struggle for power and a constant maneuvering to win the friendship of those who were, at any given moment, in power.

In 1892, the secret treaty with the Central Powers came up for renewal. Only after long heart-searching did the king decide to reveal its existence to his new ministers—but only to four of them.

Many Romanians would have looked in horror at the idea of signing a treaty with Austria-Hungary, because the ill-treatment of the Romanians in Transylvania by the ruling Magyars was becoming a burning issue. But King Carol's ministers were finally convinced that they should be protected by an alliance with Germany, and they saw this part of the treaty as the important one. So, in July 1892, the Treaty of Alliance was formally renewed. King Carol was safe from the charge of treachery to his own country. And the treaty was regularly renewed right up until World War I.

As for the issue of Transylvania itself, the conviction was growing in Bucharest that something had to be done to assist the Romanians living across the Carpathians. In 1893, the former foreign minister, Dimitrie Sturdza, addressed the Romanian Parliament with a speech that gave the world, through the publicity it received, many of the facts and figures on the situation. This occurred just before the famous trial in Cluj of the Romanians who had attempted to petition the Austrian emperor. But there was in Romania no idea of invading Transylvania. For one reason, the alliance with the Central Powers (of which Transylvania was a small part) was far too precious.

For a period in the 1890s, and again in the next decade, Dimitrie Sturdza was Romania's prime minister. But he, like many before and after him, was unable to cope satisfactorily with the insoluble problem of the government's relations with the Hungarian authorities, or to avoid the endless scandals which plagued all the governments in Bucharest.

In the beginning of our own century, new racial problems began to have political consequences: one was the fate of the "Vlachs" in Bulgaria and Macedonia, on the south side of the Danube river. But the Romanian support for these Vlachs was only a small part of a huge and complicated problem of all the various nationalities in the Balkans. The Serbs, the Greeks, the Turks, the Bulgarians, the Macedonians, and many others, were all competing for power and influence in this corner of Europe. It was part of a widespread trend in all the Continent to take pride in the qualities of one's own nation—and hence to support one's own group, right or wrong, on every issue. In the Balkans there were an enormous number of nations in a very small area.

We shall see shortly how important this national pride became. Meanwhile, in Romania, there was a terrible reminder that all the economic progress of the last half century, and all the political to-ing and fro-ing, had quite ignored and bypassed the great mass of the people, the peasants.

In March 1907, a great peasant revolt broke out in Moldavia. It soon spread all over the country. The revolt started as an anti-Jewish demonstration, because it was the Jews who were generally the middlemen, whom the peasants saw as taking away their earnings. But it rapidly turned against landlords too, especially those who rarely came to their estates but simply took away the profits. It was almost a civil war. At first, the army couldn't cope with the rioters, although the government gave it strict orders to repress the revolt. Many of the great country houses were pulled down and burned. Bucharest was practically in a state of siege. But the guns of the regular troops were in the end too much for peasants armed mainly with scythes and knives.

It is said that at least eleven thousand peasants were killed by the army as a result of this revolt. Probably the real figure is far higher. The only positive result was that the Liberal Party adopted a program of more thorough agrarian reform than before. There was a growing belief among the politicians that the lot of the peasants could no longer simply be ignored. It was still a long time, however, before the peasants felt the benefits of this reform or of the great industrial expansion that was taking place in Romania as in the whole of Europe and the United States.

But we must return to the wider crisis in the Balkans. For it is this that in the end sparked off World War I, which brought so many changes to Europe, not least to Romania.

One of the most important elements in the complicated history of the Balkans at this time was the feud between Austria-Hungary and Serbia, stemming from the Serbian desire for independence and wider influence. Austria-Hungary believed that Bulgaria could be a useful ally, since she too was hostile to Serbia. This aroused the suspicions of Bulgaria's northern neighbor, Romania. The power of Bulgaria was already increased because of internal struggles in the Turkish Empire during the so-called Young Turk revolution. Romania was afraid of further Bulgarian expansion. But then, in March 1912, Serbia and Bulgaria announced that they themselves had concluded a treaty with a view to making joint preparations for defense against, or attack on, Turkey. There was also a defensive agreement against Austria-Hungary and against Romania. Most importantly, as far as Austria-Hungary was concerned, the treaty was drawn up under the direction of that huge potential enemy, Russia.

Later in the same year, 1912, a war did break out between Turkey and the joint forces of Serbia, Bulgaria, and Greece (for Greece had also come to sign the treaty). The war did not involve Russia or Romania, and, to the great surprise of everybody, the result was a complete and sudden rout of the Turks. This upset all sorts of European diplomatic calculations. It also made the Balkan countries full of ideas of expanding their own territories. Austria-Hungary feared even more now the expansion of Serbia. By refusing to allow Serbia to have an outlet on the Adriatic Sea, she deliberately turned Serbia's expansion drive south and west—that is, against her former ally, Bulgaria.

In all this confusion Romania, too, was hoping to gain. Austria-Hungary needed her services as an ally. But at the London Peace Conference, called to settle the First Balkan War, negotiations for the return of some of the territory conceded earlier to Bulgaria broke down completely. This issue was only a small eddy in the whirlpool of international diplomacy at a time when national passions, on all sides, were growing more wild and unreasonable every day. Both Romania and Bulgaria rejected an apparently reasonable independent settlement of their border dispute. At the same time, Austria-Hungary was quarreling with Serbia, while Romania was hoping to ally herself with Serbia as a protection against Bulgaria. Clearly the situation was becoming impossibly confused.

Then Bulgaria suddenly attacked Serbia and Greece—which at once fought back. A Romanian army soon crossed southward over the Danube. From the south, the Turks advanced into Bulgaria. Bulgaria appealed desperately for help from Austria-Hungary. It was no good. She had badly miscalculated, and soon she had to agree to all the demands of her neighbors, including Romania. In August 1913, after a short conference in Bucharest, the Second Balkan War was brought to an end.

The problem now was no longer Bulgarian expansion, but Serbian. The Central Powers were worried that Serbia was becoming too powerful to control. They needed Romania as a firm ally against this power. But the thorny question of the treatment of the Romanians in Hungarian-controlled Transylvania meant that they could hardly rely on her. The tension between Bucharest and Budapest over Transylvania was stronger than ever.

One man who supported the Romanians' claim for full rights in Transylvania—admittedly from the point of view of the political ad-

vantages to Austria of a grateful Romania—was the crown prince of
Austria, the Archduke Franz Ferdinand. But, as we saw, the archduke
was assassinated by a Serbian terrorist. The Romanians had lost a
strong supporter of their cause. The wider results are well known: the
Austrian ultimatum to Serbia, the taking of sides by the European
powers, and war.

When war broke out later in the summer of 1914, Romania was
quite unable to decide on which side to range herself. On the one
hand, there was still the secret alliance with Austria-Hungary and
Germany; on the other, there was the distrust of Hungary because of
Transylvania and the fear of an alliance between the Central Powers
and Bulgaria.

On August 3, 1914, in the king's Carpathian palace in Sinaia, a
famous meeting was held at which King Carol, his ministers, and
the leading figures of the opposition were all present. This "Crown
Council" was summoned to decide the role that Romania should play
in the war. King Carol himself pressed for Romania to join the
Central Powers against Russia—partly because of the secret treaty, and
partly because of his German blood, and partly too because he thought
he was backing the winning side. All the ministers except one dis-
agreed. Many, of course, did not know about the treaty beforehand.
They feared the people would not tolerate an order to fight alongside
Hungary. The king was overruled. Romania stayed neutral.

The Romanians from Transylvania, however, were in the thick of
the struggle. They were used more or less as cannon fodder by the
Austro-Hungarian army. At first they welcomed the chance to fight
the Russians, and expected their fellow Romanians from over the Carpathians to join them. But soon they became disillusioned.

In October 1914, King Carol of Romania died. He was succeeded
by his nephew, Ferdinand, a weaker and less politically aware personality.

Meanwhile Romania was negotiating feverishly with both sides in

Royal castle in the heart of the Carpathian Mountains.

the great world conflict. By one she was offered this concession, by the other that concession; Transylvania, Bucovina, Bessarabia, all were used as tempting bait if only Romania would join this side or that. But Romania still kept out of the war, watching its ebb and flow, and building up her national resources on the strength of sales of oil and grain.

In the fall of 1915, the Central Powers were doing well on the eastern front; Bulgarian and German troops overran Serbia. Romania felt more and more isolated. But it was not until the following summer that the moment of truth arrived. Clearly the devious neutrality of Prime Minister Ionel Bratianu (son of Ion Bratianu) could last no more. In the end he came down against the Central Powers and on the side of the "Entente," which included Russia, France, and Britain.

The reason for this was clear: Romania was promised the entire territory of Transylvania (and even a small part of Hungary). On August 27, 1916, the Crown Council met once again. This time—secret treaty or no—Romania declared war on Austria-Hungary and Germany.

7

Between the Wars

Only one thing about World War I went right for Romania. She backed what in the end proved to be the winning side. Her own military fortunes were extremely unhappy. An advance into Transylvania was ignominiously thrown back, Wallachia was occupied, there was inefficiency—and even cases of treachery—in the Romanian army, and the Russians were halfhearted with their assistance. Romania's gold and official documents from the archives were sent to Moscow for safekeeping and never returned when the Bolsheviks took over there.

By 1916, however, Austria-Hungary was showing signs of exhaustion. In November, the Austrian Emperor Franz Joseph died. The new emperor, Charles, was less experienced and surrounded himself by men less suited to wage a major war.

During a pause in the campaign, the Romanian army was re-equipped and reorganized by a French general; then the fighting began again in the summer of 1917. The Romanian army distinguished itself at the battles of Marasti and Marasesti (in southern Moldavia), but the Allies' eastern front was collapsing because of the disintegration of Russian resistance. By now the revolution in Russia was under way, and Russian troops were deserting by the thousands. The only surprise was that the ordinary *Romanian* soldiers—peasants to a man

—did not fall under the Soviet revolutionary influence. One reason was the promise made by King Ferdinand to give the peasants land once the war was over, a promise confirmed by the Romanian government meeting in Iaşi, only a few miles from the front line.

When the new (Soviet) Russia sued for peace with the Central Powers, Romania had no option except to do the same.

The surrender terms were hard on Romania. They meant the loss of the Dobrogea (the land along the Black Sea coast); adjustment of the frontier along the Carpathians to suit the Hungarians; and economic exploitation by the Central Powers. But there was one advantage. Romania was allowed to carry on with the reunion of Bessarabia into Moldavia, as it used to be before Russian annexation. Already the Romanian army had gone into Bessarabia to chase out the Bolesheviks who had themselves attacked the new "Romanian" government in the Bessarabian capital of Chişinau (or Kishinev).

The man now made prime minister of Romania, Alexander Marghiloman, was a keen supporter of the Central Powers. Nevertheless, he refused to agree to all the terms of surrender—and a compromise on some details was reached in the final Treaty of Bucharest, signed on May 7, 1918. The terms of the peace meant complete dependence on Germany and Austria-Hungary. It was a national humiliation.

Meanwhile, life for the Romanians of Transylvania was as hard as ever. Many, especially priests and schoolteachers, had been imprisoned, or had fled, or had been compelled to fight in the front line for the Austro-Hungarian army.

But events in Europe generally were soon to come to the aid of the Romanians both in Transylvania and in the United Kingdom of Wallachia and Moldavia. As the Central Powers began to suffer military defeat, so all the national groups which made up the Austro-Hungarian Empire demanded more and more insistently their independence. Guerrilla organizations sprang up in all parts of the empire. People in Vienna were starving. Austria-Hungary was disintegrating. There was an attempt to make a separate peace with the Allies, but it was too late.

The Romanian leaders in Transylvania declared they would no longer recognize Hungarian domination. They took as their platform the policy proposed by United States President Wilson: "national self-determination"—the right of each ethnic group to determine its own destiny.

The Austro-Hungarian Empire was now fast dissolving. In Transylvania. Romanians seized power for themselves in several areas. On December 1, 1918, a national assembly met at Alba Iulia—rather like in the revolution of 1848—and acclaimed the union of all the Romanians. The Hungarians were powerless to resist.

With Germany defeated in the west, the United Kingdom of Wallachia and Moldavia was itself able once more to be free. The army of occupation retreated.

At the European Peace Conference which followed, Romania was represented by the new prime minister, Ionel Bratianu. Bratianu, how-

The city of Alba Iulia.

ever, was a rigid patriot, and, in the bargaining that came with the peace, he was quite unable to accept the need to make concessions. He was backed in his demands by a wildly and excessively patriotic public opinion at home. In the end, the Great Powers decided on a reasonable frontier for the new "Greater Romania," which took into account the proper claims of the Hungarians, Serbs, Bulgarians, Ukrainians, and others. Bratianu protested that he had not been consulted in these decisions, but in vain. He also resented, more reasonably, some of the other conditions laid down by the Great Powers, such as the instruction to the Romanian army to disarm.

Now Hungary became once more the focus of attention. In Budapest, a new revolutionary régime was forming out of the chaos, led by Bela Kun. His aim was both a Soviet-style government and the rescue of Hungary's power from the ruins. In the summer of 1919, his forces clashed with the Romanian army. This led quickly to the Romanian occupation of Budapest, and there began a hard period of retaliation against the Magyars. A great deal of material was seized. The complaints of the Great Powers were ignored. But neither King Ferdinand nor the Romanian government could flout the wishes of the Allies forever, and the army withdrew. By now the necessary peace agreements had all been signed, including, in June 1920, the formal union of Transylvania and Romania. And so began an uneasy interwar period, dominated first by the reconstruction of a war-torn and newly united country, then by the pressing problems of peasant poverty and the claims of the national minorities—the exact reverse of the previous Transylvanian situation—and finally by the world economic crisis which had a series of devastating effects on Romania.

"Greater Romania" was not at first sight a naturally harmonious state. The old kingdom, with Turkish and Greek traditions, was the focal point; then there was Magyar-dominated Transylvania; Austrian-controlled Bucovina; the unhappy province of Bessarabia, repressed for over a century by Russian tsarist rule; and the largely Serbian and

"Swabian" (German) Banat in the southwest corner. All this was not easy to govern as one. At the same time Romania was undergoing rapid social change. The great boyars of the past were becoming small landowners, and the peasants were beginning to play a role in politics. The widening of the franchise—which meant that at least some of the peasants had the vote—spelled the end of the Conservative Party, the party of the old boyars or landlords. There was now a bigger intellectual class, which included some who were born of peasant stock, and a small, but increasingly important middle class, consisting of business and professional men, especially lawyers.

For the first eight years or so, the country was ruled by the old "Liberals." The Liberal Party, in spite of its name, was composed mainly of upper-class landlords and businessmen of conservative views, who believed in industrialization at the expense of almost everything else. The gradual process of social change went on almost in spite of the government. This is not to say that the voice of the peasants went unheard altogether. The leader of the Peasant Party, Ion Mihalache, was a well-known and respected character. He always dressed, even at fashionable parties, in the white wool trousers and costume of the Romanian peasant. Mihalache fought for cooperation among the peasants, and the complete destruction of the large estates. But many of the other Peasant Party leaders forgot about the day-to-day aspirations of the peasants and become absorbed by their own struggle for political power in Bucharest.

Today the communist government claims that the years immediately after World War I were a time of the growing power of the workers as well as of the peasants. It is true that there were many strikes in protest against the bad conditions of the workers, including a general strike in 1920, but the power of the workers against the government was very small. Romania was still very much an agricultural country, and industry played only a minor part in the country's fortunes. It was mainly the workers on the railroads, as well as those in the growing petroleum industry and the printers, who played an active role, and their numbers were small. Even as late as 1938, the entire oil industry employed less than 25,000 workers.

The Romanian Communist Party between the wars led a hard life. It was banned in 1924, and afterward came so much under the influence of the Soviet Union that it put forward policies—such as the return of Bessarabia to the Soviet Union—that won it very little popular support. Later we shall see that, after World War II, the Communist Party of Romania was brought to power entirely because of the power of the victorious Soviet Union.

As for the government—more precisely, governments—they were preoccupied in the first of the interwar years by the long-standing problem of land reform. The great majority of Romanians were peasants. The villages were poor, dusty or muddy depending on the season, and few of the people who lived in the country were healthy or educated enough to survive and prosper in the world at large. Many of the peasants in the poorer areas—like Bessarabia—were dressed entirely in rags. Few could ever earn enough money to buy tools to work the land more efficiently and escape the vicious circle of poverty.

But the governments did not forget the promises made in the war. A large amount of land was taken away from the big landowners and distributed to those who owned least. But the process was slow, and there was a great deal of corruption. Besides, many of the small holdings that the peasants received were too small for them to make a profit. Much of the land was suffering from centuries of neglect and in need of irrigation. Many of the peasants emigrated to the United States or to western European countries during these years.

Unfortunately, in Romania, sympathy with the peasant sometimes went hand in hand with an extreme patriotism and also with anti-Semitism. Many Romanians thought of Jews as people who exploited the peasants, who ran the industry of the country, and who made deals with the government at the expense of the peasants.

In 1923, an organization called the "League of Christian Defense" was founded; it attracted a number of young supporters such as Corneliu Codreanu. Codreanu in turn created a similar youth organization, called the "Legion of the Archangel Michael"; it was this organization which later produced the "Iron Guard," a name that became associated with fascism in Romania.

The "Guardists" claimed to defend the historic values of the peasants and would march about the streets wearing green shirts, with little bags of Romanian soil around their necks, denouncing all that they considered foreign—especially the Jews. They had a great appeal among the simple peasants with their promise to do away with the corruption of the politicians. The Guardists were responsible for the murder of several politicians who opposed them. Codreanu was a keen supporter of Hitler, who came to power with his Nazis in Germany in 1933.

These political movements—fascist, communist, and others too—developed against a background of traditional government by the Liberal Party, with intervals of power in the hands of the National Peasant Party. At the same time there was a series of crises concerning the monarchy. The son of King Ferdinand and Queen Marie, Prince Carol, became involved in a scandal with a certain Madame Lupescu. When out of the country with his mistress, Carol was informed by King Ferdinand that he refused to allow him back unless he returned alone. Carol decided to stay away, and in 1925 abdicated in favor of his small son, Michael. The National Peasant Party claimed they had not even been consulted on these matters of importance and attacked the Liberal government strongly. They used this opportunity to win support and, at the end of 1928, soon after the death of King Ferdinand, their leader, Iuliu Maniu, became prime minister.

Although the National Peasant Party attracted some foreign money into Romania to help build up industries, their record was otherwise disappointing. In spite of their name, they did no more to help the peasants than the Liberals. The depression which followed the great Wall Street crash in 1929 soon began to have an effect in Romania, as the price of grain fell. That made the government less popular than ever. But the National Peasant Party fell from power in the end for precisely the same reason that the Liberals had fallen before—the question of the monarchy. In 1930, Carol suddenly returned to Romania. Maniu, to preserve the dynasty, supported Carol's claim to return to the throne and become king. But he insisted that Carol should not bring his mistress Madame Lupescu into the country. When the king did just that, Maniu resigned.

From now until the outbreak of World War II the king played the key role in Romania. King Carol was an energetic and vain man who loved power and the trappings of power. He was no great intellect and was liable to be carried away by his own eloquence. The Romanians had a proverb: "The fish grows rotten from the head"—in other

King Carol II. (Credit: Radio Times Hulton Picture Library)

words, corruption at the top is the cause of a corrupt society. Carol and his courtiers must bear the main responsibility for the decline of Romanian government and society in the 1930s.

The prime minister of King Carol's first government was his old tutor—and a world-famous historian—Nicolae Iorga. There soon followed, however, a new period of government by the National Peasants, and then by the Liberals who (especially when Tatarescu was prime minister) were more and more under the king's influence. During this period there was growing unrest from the right and the left, that is to say from the Iron Guardists and the communists. In 1933, for instance, there was a violent strike in the railway yards in the suburbs of Bucharest, which led to the death of many workers; in the same year, the Guardists murdered a Liberal prime minister.

King Carol decided to found his own patriotic movement to challenge the Iron Guard. Codreanu, the Guardist leader, was arrested and imprisoned. Later, he and other eminent Guardists were "shot while trying to escape." In 1938, after a complicated series of political maneuvers, by which the king split the forces of the leading political parties, he founded a new "Front of National Renaissance." It was a patriotic movement, with the patriarch of the Orthodox Church as prime minister, but not so extreme as the Iron Guard. From now on, with the king taking over the role of dictator, and the economic situation desperate, Romania began to come more and more under German influence.

After World War I, with Germany and Austria-Hungary defeated, Romania made a pact with Yugoslavia and Czechoslovakia (called the Little Entente), and this pact had the support of France. German influence was nil. Romania also took part in a round of conferences and treaties with Greece, Turkey, and Bulgaria which, for the first time in history, appeared to give the strife-torn Balkan corner of Europe a hope of unity and stability for the future. But it was not to be. The power of Hitler, who destroyed the Little Entente when he invaded Czechoslovakia in 1938, was in the end too great.

Nazi Germany had particular interests in Romania, oil and grain. The Romanian oil fields were a prize that Germany desperately wanted to win if she was going to expand toward the east: in other words, conquer Poland and the Soviet Union, as well as Czechoslovakia and Austria. Ever since the beginning of the 1930s, Germany had worked her way into a strong position as far as the Romanian economy was concerned. Germany offered Romania better prices than any other country for the things she had to sell. More and more it was German advice on how to run the Romanian economy that was taken.

In August 1939, Hitler signed his notorious pact with Stalin, and Romania was once again caught like a nut in a nutcracker between the great powers of Germany and Russia.

In September 1939, World War II began. Great Britain and France had guaranteed the independence of both Poland and Romania, as well as Greece. When Germany invaded Poland, war was at once declared. At first, because of the Nazi-Soviet Pact, Hitler did not move farther east. But the Soviet Union moved west—also because of the Pact—into "her half" of Poland.

As far as Romania was concerned, this cynical Pact, between two countries which hated each other and were soon to be at war, could scarcely have been more damaging. In a secret clause, Germany gave a free hand to the Soviet Union to reclaim Bessarabia; the Soviet Union had never recognized Romania's right to possess it. Germany expressed her "complete political disinterestedness" in the area.

On June 26, 1940, the Soviet Union suddenly presented an ultimatum to Romania demanding not only Bessarabia, but also the northern half of Bucovina, which had never been under Russian rule (it was directly under Austrian control between 1775 and 1918). The Germans advised Romania to accept. There was no option but to do so. Popular feeling became more anti-Soviet than ever. The Iron Guardists were pardoned by the king, and pro-Germans came to power in the Romanian government.

But the dismembering of Romania had not yet finished. Bulgaria demanded, and received, the southern part of the Dobrogea, which had been taken over by Romania after the Second Balkan War in 1913. Then, worst of all, Hungary demanded back large parts of Transylvania. The dispute was "settled" by representatives of the German and Italian governments in Vienna. A line was drawn through the middle of Transylvania; the northern and eastern parts, including the capital city Cluj, were awarded to Hungary. The scenes in Transylvania which followed were horrifying. Romanians fled from the north, carrying whatever they could lay their hands on. The Magyars in the south were chased out of their homes. There was hatred and persecution on both sides.

In September 1940, as a result of this crisis, King Carol abdicated. Once again the young King Michael came to the throne. Carol and his mistress, Madame Lupescu, left Bucharest in a train riddled with bullets fired by the triumphant Iron Guardists. General Ion Antonescu was now prime minister, and the Iron Guard leader, Horia Sima, his deputy.

In October, German troops entered Romania, to "train" the Romanian army. Even so, the violently pro-Nazi Iron Guardists were not satisfied. They began to commit a series of massacres and outrages, especially against Jews. They seemed to want, as it were, to out-Nazi the Nazis. They kidnapped, then brutally murdered the famous historian and one-time prime minister, Nicolae Iorga. Prime Minister Antonescu was forced to react against this threat to public order. In this he was supported by the German authorities, for the Germans were more interested in Romania's oil and grain than in violence, even violence in support of their own ideas. After a particularly bloody slaughter of Jews, the Guardists were confronted with the combined force of the Romanian and German armies and were crushed. Now Romania was firmly in the grip of the right-wing, but less extreme *"Conducator"* (leader, or "Führer") General Ion Antonescu. The opposition leaders inside Romania (including such men as Iuliu Maniu) remained silent and impotent.

On June 22, 1941, the Romanian army crossed the Soviet frontier, at the same moment as the fateful German offensive was launched. In a short time, Bessarabia and northern Bucovina were back in Romanian hands.

8

The New Order

If only the Romanian army had halted at the River Dniester when Bessarabia had been recaptured. But it was not to be, and the army, under strong German pressure, pushed on into the Russian heartlands. It set up a very corrupt administration in the southwest corner of the Soviet Union, calling it "Transnistria" (across the Dniester). From now on, Romania depended on the success of the German army in conquering the Soviet Union. When in 1943 the turning point was reached, and the German advance halted at Stalingrad and Moscow, the consequences were as dire for Romania as they were for Nazi Germany.

In Romania, the government and the German authorities were not on the customary friendly terms of allies: the Romanians felt the Germans were exploiting them, taking their resources and using their manpower. Besides, the Germans kept in Berlin the chiefs of the Iron Guard, ready to replace Antonescu's government if he did not cooperate. The Romanians also resented the continuing Hungarian control of northern Transylvania, which was an obsession with them throughout the war.

As for Romanian opposition, or resistance, it was quite ineffectual. Maniu and Bratianu, leaders of the National Peasant and Liberal parties, acted as a sort of "tolerated" opposition, but their influence was small. Like perhaps the majority of the Romanian people, they felt that Romania had no quarrel with Britain, France, or the United States, but only with the Soviet Union. Several attempts were made to make a separate peace with the western Allies.

In the summer of 1944, the tide of war had completely turned. Romania was making desperate efforts to make peace. American and British bombers were attacking the oilfields. Romania would willingly have surrendered, but for the threat of a Soviet occupation.

Finally, the realities of war, and the exposed position of Romania in eastern Europe, could no longer be ignored. On August 23, 1944, young King Michael arrested General Antonescu and declared that the war against the Allies was over and that a new government, including many members of the opposition, was to be formed. Shortly afterward, Romania declared war on Germany. Romanian troops began to march against the Germans and the Hungarians on their western flank. In this final campaign, Romania suffered 170,000 casualties.

From now on, Soviet influence in Romania was all-powerful. The

Romanian soldiers crossing the Tisa River into Hungary, October 1944.

western Allies recognized their inability to alter the course of events. Taking advantage of this free hand, the Soviet Union, after fighting alongside Romanian troops up until the end of the war in Europe, then demanded huge sums of money as reparations, and, far more important, dictated the way that Romania should now be run.

Although the communist government in Romania today claims that the abrupt turnaround in Romanian policy in August 1944 was due to the efforts of the Romanian communists themselves, this is clearly untrue. The decision was taken by the king, and approved by the whole of the Romanian opposition. The number of communists involved was too small to be significant.

But in October 1944, the Social Democrats, together with a peasant organization called the Ploughmen's Front and other left-wing organizations, split from the National Peasant and Liberal parties and formed the National Democratic Front. In this the communists did play an important part. The National Democratic Front was far more active than its rivals in campaigning against the pro-Germans in top positions in the country. This was the party which the Russians used first to gain control. Communists were appointed to as many key posts as possible. Protests against the old politicians were stepped up. Every method of intimidation was used. On one notorious occasion, when King Michael hesitated to obey a Soviet demand that a minister should be dismissed, Soviet Deputy Commissar Andrei Vyshinski gave the king a couple of hours to change his mind, pounded his fist on the table, and stalked out of the room, slamming the door so hard that the plaster cracked.

By March 1945, a new government under Petru Groza, the Ploughmen's Front leader, and including a gang of discredited and unscrupulous politicians of the old parties, came to power. It was a further step along the road to the communization of Romania.

The war leaders, among them General Antonescu, were tried and executed. As Soviet pressure built up, King Michael retired to his

Communist rally, toward the end of World War II.

summer castle at Sinaia and refused to sign any decrees. There were international protests, but to no avail. An American journalist, Mark Ethridge, was dispatched by the United States to report on the situation. As a result, the Russians agreed to a few formal compromises, and the Western Powers recognized the new Russian-sponsored government in Romania. The Peace Treaty, signed in February 1947, gave final and formal recognition to the new régime.

During the course of that year, the various opposition elements, including Maniu and Mihalache, were rounded up and arrested. Three Moscow-trained communists, Ana Pauker, Vasile Luca, and Emil Bodnaraş, took over key posts in the National Democratic Front government. Ana Pauker was already a notorious figure. A rabbi's daughter, she married in the 1920s a leading communist, only to betray him to Stalin's secret police when they had both fled to the Soviet Union. Returning to Romania, Ana Pauker was arrested, but freed in 1940 in an exchange of political prisoners with the Soviet Union. She returned, along with many Romanian communists, in the wake of the Red Army in 1944. She was a colorful, but much feared personality in the new régime.

In December 1947, the new communist-dominated government called on King Michael to abdicate, and he was sent into exile. Today the ex-king lives and works in Switzerland.

So ended a dynasty and an epoch. Romania was now a republic. And from a tiny party with a membership of less than 1,000 in 1944, the Communist Party of Romania, expanded out of all recognition, had taken over the complete control of the country. At first it depended on Soviet backing; but in later years, as we shall see, it shook itself free from direct Soviet control.

The late 1940s and the 1950s—the Stalinist period—were particularly hard times in Romania. The people suffered both economically and socially. Much of the country's produce was delivered to the Soviet Union as compensation for war damage. Although Romanians and Russians had fought side by side for the last part of the war and the Romanians had formed a communist government in accordance with the Soviet Union's plans, the country was treated worse than any other Soviet satellite once the war was over. One particularly effective means of extracting money from the country was the so-called Joint Soviet-Romanian companies—"Sov-Roms." These companies had a Russian chairman, but were financed by Romanian capital. The profits were "divided"; that is to say, one half went directly to the Soviet Union and the other half was claimed as war reparations. In January 1949, Romania became a member of COMECON, the economic grouping of the European communist countries, cutting her off from western aid and western markets. On Romania's behalf, the Soviet Union declined the offer of Marshall Aid—American funds to help postwar reconstruction.

In the early days of communist rule, all land, industries, banks, and so on were taken over by the state. Even small businesses were taken from their owners. Everyone became employees of the state. Grandiose economic plans were drawn up but they couldn't be fullfilled, in spite of harsh discipline, because of Soviet exploitation. Only toward the middle of the 1950s did Romanian industry begin to develop more satisfactorily.

According to classic Marxist-Leninist principles, agriculture had to take second place to industry. Very little money was spent on the farms. Already in 1948, the process of collectivization began. Small holdings and farms were merged into huge agricultural units owned collectively by the peasants. The Soviet model was followed closely. Most of the peasants resisted collectivization. Although their methods of cultivation had always been primitive and inefficient, they took great pride in their small plots. But they could not hold up the drive toward collectivization. It was a long process, but by 1961 it was completed.

The entire population was subject to the harshest discipline. Those of bourgeois origin—the aristocracy, the middle classes, rich peasants, and so on—suffered intense persecution. Labor camps were filled with prisoners. Thousands of political prisoners were executed. Many lost their lives when forced to cut the reeds in the Danube delta in terrible conditions; others suffered while working on a huge and futile project, building a canal between the Black Sea and the Danube to bypass the delta.

The churches too were persecuted. The Greco-Roman (Uniate) Church, founded at the end of the seventeenth century as a combination of Orthodoxy and Roman Catholicism, was banned altogether. Priests of all denominations were imprisoned. As in the Soviet Union, atheist propaganda poured off the state-owned presses.

This was a dark and dreary period of Romanian history. The secret police filled the people with fear. They were afraid to talk to each other. The people resented the control of the Communist Party and there were few points of contact between the rulers and the ruled. Foreigners seldom visited the country. From the point of view of the

Western world, Romania had disappeared behind the Iron Curtain.

At the head of the new régime was the General Secretary of the Communist Party, Gheorghe Gheorghiu-Dej, a veteran of prewar strikes (he was imprisoned after the 1933 Grivița railway strike). Gheorghiu-Dej was a native Romanian, whose political experience had been gained entirely in his own country. From the beginning, however, he was faced with a conflict between the Romanian element in the party and those trained in Moscow, many of whom were also of Jewish or Hungarian origin. The conflict was resolved in the early fifties, with the purge of Ana Pauker and her colleagues. In 1961, Gheorghiu-Dej claimed that, with this purge, he had begun the process of "de-Stalinization," even before the death of the Soviet dictator.

In 1955, Romania joined the Warsaw Pact, the communist military alliance designed to counteract the North Atlantic Treaty Organization, NATO. The alliance included all the members of the European Soviet bloc, Poland, East Germany, Czechoslovakia, Hungary, Bulgaria, and Albania. Yugoslavia was not a member, since in 1948 she had broken away from the Soviet bloc and had begun the search for her own brand of socialism. Albania was later to leave the Warsaw Pact also, as a result of the quarrel between the Soviet Union and the People's Republic of China, when Albania became identified with the Chinese point of view.

In the fall of 1956, there were massive revolts against Soviet control in both Poland and Hungary. Only in Hungary, however, were Soviet troops and tanks called in to crush the rebellion. This was to a great extent due to the decision by Imre Nagy and the other leaders of the revolt to reject membership of the Warsaw Pact and become neutral. This was too direct a threat to Soviet security for the Russians to tolerate.

During these dramatic times, Romania was inactive. It was not in the Romanian nature—and history has provided many examples to prove it—to fight against insuperable odds. The Romanians have

seldom been pioneers of freedom, as we have seen, but progress slowly
and cautiously toward it.

There was some justification for their approach when, two years
later, in the summer of 1958, Soviet troops withdrew from Romanian
territory. It was from about this time that the story of Romania's
gradual emergence from beneath the dead weight of Soviet control
began.

The drive for national independence came into the open in the early
1960s, when Romania protested against the plans of the Soviet Party
chief, Nikita Khrushchev, to integrate the economies of the eastern
European countries. The Romanians felt that this would bring them
even more under Soviet influence, since the Soviet Union was so much
the most powerful force within COMECON, the international com-

New Romanian industry—a coke
and chemical works at Hunedoara.

munist economic organization. Besides, Romania had invested a great deal of money and resources in building up her own industries, many of which had never existed before in the country; it was feared that these might be cut back, so that the more advanced bloc countries would concentrate on industry and Romania would be left with the less profitable job of selling her agricultural produce. Fortunately for Romania, no decision could be taken in COMECON without the unanimous approval of all its members. So the integration idea was shelved. It was not for many years that the pressure to integrate was renewed.

Also in the early 1960s, a campaign of de-Russification got under way. It was unobtrusive and subtle and tightly controlled by the Communist Party. Street names were changed from the name of a Russian general to that of a Romanian historical hero; the town of Braşov, which had been named Stalin, reverted to Braşov; the center of Russian cultural activities in Bucharest was closed down, and so on.

By 1965, when Gheorghiu-Dej died, and Nicolae Ceauşescu became party leader, the first steps along the road of national independence had been taken. Ceauşescu was (and is) an ardent nationalist. It was at once apparent when he took over that the drive for independence was going to be carried on, perhaps even faster than before.

Romania was helped by the quarrel between the Soviet Union and China. She refused to take sides in this dispute, and insisted that no country should attempt to tell another how to run its affairs. It was clear all along that this principle was meant to apply to the Soviet Union's relations with Romania as much as to those with China. Romania has long insisted on the cardinal principles of "sovereignty, national independence, noninterference in the internal affairs of another country, and relations based on mutual advantage."

This policy comes close to Yugoslavia's concept of "nonalignment"—that is, freedom from either of the blocs or superpowers—although Romania is still a member of the Warsaw Pact. In the 1960s, Romania's relations with Yugoslavia became more warm and friendly than at any time in their history. A symbol of their closeness, is the great hydro-electric station, dam, and navigation channels at the Iron Gates, where the Danube River cuts through a high gorge, forming the border between the two countries. The Iron Gates, incidentally, is the point where Trajan crossed into Dacia many centuries before.

In 1967, Romania reestablished diplomatic relations with West Germany, although the Soviet Union and East Germany had strong objections. The Romanians argued that the Federal Republic of Germany was already her second largest trading partner (after the Soviet Union) and that, besides, she was free to have normal relations with any country, irrespective of its social and political system. In the same way, Romania is the only communist state to maintain relations with both Israel and the Arab states, although some Arab states broke off relations as a result.

But then, in the early hours of the morning of August 21, 1968, the situation of the Soviet bloc countries changed abruptly. The Russian army, backed up by Polish, East German, Hungarian, and Bulgarian units, invaded Czechoslovakia. Europe was suddenly in the middle of a major crisis.

The Romanian reaction was swift. On the afternoon after the invasion, a hundred thousand wildly enthusiastic people gathered in the great square between the Communist Party headquarters and the former Royal Palace, to hear Nicolae Ceausescu address them. Almost everyone there believed that the Russian troops would soon be crossing the Romanian border. Ceausescu delivered a fighting speech, promising bloody resistance to anyone who threatened Romania's national integrity; young Romanians were encouraged to join the newly formed "Patriotic Guards." Rumors of an invasion of Romania crisscrossed the towns and villages all over the country.

But, in the end, there was no invasion. The Soviet hold over Czechoslovakia tightened, and the Romanian (and Yugoslav) authorities struck a calmer note. Romania returned to her delicately balanced position between east and west, keeping her independence without provoking Soviet intervention. But one thing could not be forgotten. At the moment of danger, the Communist Party and the people had reacted as one single, patriotic unit for the first time in two decades.

Since 1968, more sober realities have reasserted themselves. For one thing, the economic situation began to deteriorate. After achieving very rapid growth indeed over a long period, as far as industry was concerned, neglect of agriculture and unwillingness to reform old-fashioned planning techniques at last began to have a telling effect. Romania has to sell large quantities of agricultural produce in order to pay for the machinery and equipment she needs—most of which has to come from the west. This has meant that the people in Romania have often had to do without much of the rich produce of the land. The situation was made worse by a disastrous series of floods in the early summer of 1970. They were the worst in the country's entire history. According to some estimates, they canceled much of the progress made in the previous five years. The floods were indeed a cruel blow. Not only did many suffer at the time, but they had serious long-term effects. Faced with economic problems and fresh memories of the invasion of Czechoslovakia, the party began to tighten its control over the population. Although the majority of political prisoners were freed by 1964, the secret police apparatus, called the *Securitate,* is still a powerful force.

The system of government by the Communist Party has changed little since its early days of power. The party is headed by its general secretary, who today, in the person of Nicolae Ceausescu, is also Head of State. Below the general secretary, at the apex of the pyramid, is an ever-widening hierarchy of party officials, from the Politburo, to the Central Committee, and down to the local party cells.

Parallel to the party hierarchy—but ultimately under party control

—is the state system of the Socialist Republic of Romania. Constitutionally, the supreme body is the Grand National Assembly. It meets only every six months, and in between times the ordinary business of government is organized by the State Council, whose members are elected by the Grand National Assembly. The Head of State is its chairman, or president. Under the supervision of the State Council is the Council of Ministers, which consists of the ministers in charge of the various functions of state and the economic sectors. Then there is the whole network of local councils in the administrative districts of Romania.

In all areas of life in modern Romania, the Communist Party is active: in schools, in the armed forces, in the trade unions and so on. Meetings to explain party decisions, or to instil a greater sense of socialism, are held frequently in places of work all over the country. It is no longer necessary to be a member of the Communist Party to gain promotion to a responsible job, but it is still a considerable advantage.

Inevitably, the people of a country which has been ruled for centuries by such men as Vlad the Impaler, or Basil the Wolf, or the succession of corrupt Phanariot princes in the period of Turkish rule, of a country whose slow attempts at modern democratic government were constantly frustrated by venal politicians and devastating wars, cannot escape the vices of the past when under the rule of the Communist Party. The rulers—no longer the prince and his boyars, but Nicolae Ceausescu and the Communist Party—still wield absolute power. In such conditions, corruption is encouraged and people are tempted to forget principles and act cynically for personal gain. Living is still a hard business in Romania. It is only natural that the people should try by any means to ease the burden of the myriad rules and regulations of an all-powerful state.

Nevertheless, the new order has done away with many of the worst abuses of the past. Social differences have been reduced. People have found again their feelings of patriotism. This was never more clearly demonstrated than at the time of the 1970 floods, when the whole people made great sacrifices to repair the damage and put the country back on its feet.

9

Hungarians, Germans, Jews, and Others

Today there are between 1,500,000 and 2,000,000 citizens of Romania who have Hungarian blood in their veins. Some of them speak scarcely any Romanian. The great majority live in Transylvania, descendants of the Magyars and the Szeklers who, as we saw earlier, dominated the province for many centuries. It's difficult to know exactly how many Hungarians there are altogether in Romania, because some have changed their names to Romanian-sounding ones. Some, too, regard themselves as equally Hungarian and Romanian in origin.

At times in history it has been only too obvious that the two groups hated each other. There are still some Hungarians who think of the Romanians over on the other side of the Carpathians as weak and corrupt; and there are some Romanians who see Hungarians as proud and obstinate. But by and large the two get on much better than they used to.

The atmosphere is completely changed, for example, in comparison with the late nineteenth or early twentieth century, when the chauvinistic Hungarian government in Budapest was in direct control of Transylvania; or between the two World Wars, when the Romanians were paying off old scores; or, especially, in 1940, when an artificial line was drawn through Transylvania, forcing the Hungarians to flee north of it, and the Romanians south.

In 1952, a Magyar Autonomous Region was created in eastern Transylvania. The Hungarians who lived there could decide local issues for themselves. But in 1968 the whole idea was dropped because there is in fact no single large area where Hungarians live and where there are not at least some Romanians, or Germans, or members of another national minority.

The most Hungarian-feeling town in Transylvania is the capital, Cluj, called in Hungarian, Kolozsvar. This is made quite clear from the street signs, which are written in both Hungarian and Romanian, or from the names above the shops; and Hungarian is the language you are most likely to hear as you stroll about the streets. The University of Cluj is a joint one now, formed by the union of the old Hungarian and Romanian universities. Courses are given in both languages. You can hear plays and operas in Hungarian at the Hungarian State Theatre and Opera House.

The buildings in Cluj, with tall stone facades, and the churches, with spiky Gothic or stern square towers, are like those you can see in Hungary itself, or in many parts of Austria and Germany. They are quite different from the Greek- and Turkish-looking houses and churches which date from the past centuries in Wallachia and Moldavia. But in the Transylvanian villages where Hungarians live, the cottages of wood or stone are not so different from those in other parts of modern Romania. This shows how strong the Romanian influence was in the countryside, whereas the Hungarian influence dominated the towns.

Since Romania regained the entire province of Transylvania in 1945, there have been two main flash points when Hungarian and Romanian national feelings have been aroused sufficiently to recall the old days when bad blood was the rule rather than the exception. One was in 1956, at the time of the Hungarian revolt against Soviet control. The Hungarians in Transylvania passionately supported their fellow Hungarians across the border and held meetings and demonstrations. But the Romanian authorities suppressed all these disturbances and in the years that followed carried out a number of arrests among Hungarians—although this was also the time when many Romanians, too, were arrested to counteract the ferment in eastern Europe that the Hungarian revolution had caused.

The second moment of tension was at the time of the Warsaw Pact invasion of Czechoslovakia in August 1968. Some Romanians feared that the Hungarians in Transylvania would take advantage of the troop movements—and of Romania's unpopularity with the Soviet Union for not taking part in the invasion—to create trouble. But the fears were groundless. Today there is more harmony between the Hungarian minority and the Romanians than ever before.

As for the Germans—descendants of the Saxons who came into Transylvania as frontier guards soon after the Szeklers, and of the Swabians who came much later—they too have their own history and traditions. One version of their first arrival in the country is that they are the people who followed the Pied Piper of Hamelin. He was the man whom, according to legend, the citizens of the German town of Hamelin employed to get rid of their plague of rats; he did this by leading them out of the town as he played his pipe. But when he was not given his reward, he punished the people of Hamelin by playing his magic pipe again, only this time it was the children who followed him. Never, it is said, did he bring them back again.

Perhaps that's why the Germans in Romania always had a reputation for miserliness—perhaps they took after their ancestors in Hamelin! Early visitors to Transylvania used to remark on the way the Saxons kept themselves to themselves: how they seldom married anyone who was not also a Saxon; and how they worked enormously hard, but hated to spend their money. It used to be said that they preferred to have only one child, so that their property would not have to be divided after their death. The Germans did not like strangers. Travelers used to say that they never received any food or lodging from the Germans in Transylvania, although the Romanians and the Hungarians there were famous for their generosity and their hospitality.

One English traveler noticed this sign hung up above the door of a German peasant's cottage, which goes—in English translation:

> Trust yourself to only one—
> 'Tis not wise to trust to none;
> Better, though, to have no friend
> Than on many to depend.

A number of the Germans in Romania at the beginning of World War II sided with Hitler's Nazis. When, in August 1944, Romania began to fight on the allied side, these Romanian Germans either fled or were captured and later expelled from the country. They left behind prosperous farms and businesses, and these were taken over by the Romanians. But, today, things are very different. The Germans who live in Romania now are peaceful and hardworking. Some have been allowed to leave and go and live in West Germany, but most have stayed. In all, there are not far short of 500,000 Romanian citizens of German origin today, the biggest German minority in any European country.

Most of the Swabians, Germans who first settled in Romania in the sixteenth century, live in the Banat, the southwest corner of Romania. The most important centers of Saxon life are the towns of Sibiu and Braşov—known in the German language as Hermannstadt and Kronstadt. Both are historic towns, Sibiu on the western side of the Carpathian Mountains, and Braşov on the eastern edge.

In Braşov, the old Merchant's Hall, which was built in the sixteenth century and served for a long time as the trading center of the guilds of (mainly Saxon) merchants, has been restored quite recently. You can see the cellars, the warehouses, and the shops and salesrooms. Many of the Saxons were involved in trade, and it was through Brașov that much of the trade between Transylvania and the principalities of Wallachia and Moldavia was done. Inside the town itself, there was a strict distinction between the Saxon and the Magyar population on the one hand, and the Romanians on the other. There is a gate in the center of the town which you can see today; through this gate no Romanian could come, for a large part of the town center was forbidden to people of Romanian blood.

German is the first language of many of the inhabitants of Brașov and Sibiu. Saxon settlers have lived in Sibiu, which is a pleasant and

A street in the town of Sibiu.

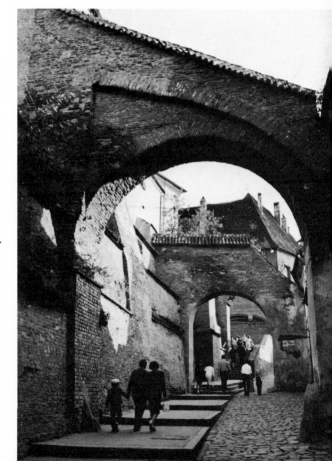

prosperous town in the very center of Romania, since the early Middle Ages. For a while, it was the military capital of Transylvania, and many of its ancient fortifications survive today. It is also the home of the Brukenthal Museum, which houses the rich art collection of a former Saxon-born governor of Transylvania, Baron Brukenthal. It includes paintings by such famous artists as Titian, Rubens, and van Dyck as well as many examples of Romanian painting and folk art.

Another town which had a considerable Saxon population is Sighişoara. One fascinating example of its rich past which still survives is the 200-foot high clock tower, built in the fourteenth century. In 1648 a local craftsman put in the tower a marvelous mechanism that tells the day of the week every midnight, when a carved figure emerges from the tower.

Bistriţa is a town in northern Transylvania which also had a large Saxon colony (incidentally, it also marked the northernmost point of the ancient Kingdom of Dacia). For years, Bistriţa was a center of commerce between Transylvania and Moldavia—although the route between them lay over the high pass known as the Tihuta Pass. All these towns look, at least in parts, very like towns in Germany, Austria, or other countries which once were part of the Austrian and Hungarian empires.

The Saxon villages in Romania, which cluster round Braşov and Sibiu and elsewhere, have a special look about them. They are always spotlessly clean, and the houses form a continuous row along the street, joined by a big porchlike gate made of brick or stone. The houses usually have three windows which face the road—unlike Romanian cottages which, by tradition, are built sideways on.

Today there are far fewer Jews in Romania than there used to be. A hundred years or so ago, there were probably about 500,000 in Wallachia and Moldavia alone, and half the population of the Moldavian capital of Iaşi was Jewish. Just before World War II, there were over 800,000 Jews in Greater Romania. Of course they suffered a great deal during the war, although the Romanians did not treat them as Hitler's Nazis treated the Jews. The extreme brutality of the Iron Guards was never adopted as the country's official policy, and it evoked the disapproval of most ordinary Romanians.

In the nineteenth century, Jews were not given ordinary rights as citizens. As discussed earlier, this became an international scandal, and many western European statesmen protested against anti-Semitism in Romania. Visitors to Romania were often shocked by the terrible poverty in which whole communities of Jews lived. But that is something you will not see today.

When the communists took over in Romania at the end of World War II, many of the leading figures (such as Ana Pauker) were Jews. It was felt by the Soviet leaders that, after the immense suffering of the Jewish people in Europe during the war, the survivors could be relied upon to be firmly antifascist. In this calculation they were correct, but unfortunately these Jewish communists in Romania became identified by the people with the harsh years of the imposition of communism under Soviet domination. This reinforced a common, historic reluctance to accept the Jews in Romania as citizens with equal rights.

Many Romanian Jews have left the country since the war to go to Israel. This has been one cause of the fact that relations between Romania and Israel have been closer than those between Israel and other communist states. But many—about 100,000—still live in Romania, practicing their religion freely, under the guidance of a jovial Chief Rabbi, who is also a member of the Romanian parliament.

If anything, the Gypsies in Romania were treated even worse than the Jews. Until 1848, most Gypsies were slaves, working usually as the servants of boyar families. Even after they were freed, their condition remained in most cases exactly the same.

One legend has it that there were Gypsies in Dacia at the time the Roman Emperor Trajan crossed the Danube in A.D. 106. It is more likely that they came into eastern Europe in the eleventh century, or maybe a little earlier. Their origin is still obscure and buried in myth. Some say that they came from India, others from Lower Egypt.

Whatever is the truth, a recognizable and quite separate ethnic group called the Gypsies did make their way into Romania many centuries ago and have been there ever since. Traditionally, they kept themselves alive by tinkering, horse-trading, playing the fiddle, telling fortunes, or else simply cheating and stealing, always living from hand to mouth. But it was only in Romania, out of all the countries in Europe where Gypsies have lived, that they were forced to be slaves.

Not all of them, of course, were trapped like that. Many lived on the edges of towns and villages, or kept up a wandering life all over the country. Some tried to make a fortune in the gold mines in the Carpathians—but without success.

The Gypsies have never believed in private property. They have never had any wish to burden themselves with a house or possessions. They are most of all interested in their own personal freedom. Alexander Cuza, the first prince of the United Principalities of Wallachia and Moldavia, made a special law to take into account the Gypsies' love of freedom. He decreed that all men should get five years in prison for stealing a horse—*except* a nomad Gypsy; h⌐ should get only three months for the same offense. That, Cuza reckoned, was the equivalent sentence for someone who prized his freedom so highly.

Until World War II, there were up to about 200,000 Gypsies in Romania; now there are only about half that number. Today they are treated like any other Romanian citizen, although they still look very distinctive. They wear their bright, multicolored clothes, and indeed they still do many of the traditional jobs. The Gypsies have special permission to sell flowers in the towns, and you can see them on many a street corner in Bucharest, squatting on the pavement, surrounded by buckets full of bunches of flowers. Many Gypsies have been housed in modern apartment buildings nowadays, but they do not

all appreciate this introduction to twentieth-century living as much as other Romanians.

And then there are all the other people of various origins who live in modern Romania. There are the Serbs, who live, like the Swabian Germans, mainly in the southwest part of the country (the Banat); and the Russians, who live mainly on the Black Sea coast (as do the Tatars); and the Ukrainians, Ruthenians, Bulgarians, and Czechs and Slovaks and so on. In fact Romania is rather like a museum—a living museum—of European peoples. In unexpected places all over the country, you can find a small colony of people, living perhaps in one village, who are, say, Bulgarian to a man. Or they may be of another origin. Always there is a story behind their presence there.

Doi Mai, for example, is a little fishing village (and now a summer resort) down on the Black Sea coast near the Bulgarian border. Today there lives in Doi Mai (which means the second of May) a small colony of a special religious sect known as Lipovani. One day, many years ago, they set out from the Ukraine, where they had been persecuted for their beliefs. They were looking for a quiet spot to settle and, on their way down the coast, one of their carts collapsed. They had to stay overnight. When they woke up, these tall bearded men and their families liked the place so much that they stayed. The date that the cart broke down was the second of May, and that explains the name of the village.

It is frequently difficult for people of differing racial and ethnic backgrounds to live together without friction. But the Romanian government has tried to achieve harmony. It has a policy today of treating all citizens of whatever origin as equal. There has been too much trouble from national tensions in the past, not only in Romania but in the whole Balkan region of Europe, for the lesson of tolerance not to have made a mark.

10

Religion and Art

Religion has always played a key role in the history of the Romanian lands. In Transylvania, there were constant tensions between the Roman Catholics and the Protestants—with pressure from the Austrian government to adopt the Catholic religion. There was also a refusal of the ruling groups—the Hungarians and the Saxons—to recognize the Orthodox religion, which was the faith of almost the entire Romanian people in the province (and also, of course, in Wallachia and Moldavia). In 1699, the Uniate Church was formed, again under Austrian pressure, to bring the Orthodox believers under Roman Catholic control. But, as we saw, this "Greco-Catholic" faith was dissolved when the communists came to power in 1948.

Religious faith was closely identified with nationality, and the persecution of one church by another followed the pattern of tensions between the peoples in the Romanian lands.

Christianity became established in Wallachia and Moldavia some time after the tenth century, although it had penetrated fitfully north of the Danube many centuries before. At this time it was associated with the Slavonic rite, and the connection with the church in Bulgaria was particularly close. The language of the Church was Slavonic, and it was not until much later that Romanian was used.

Today Romania is officially an atheistic state. In the early years of communism, this meant that all religions were persecuted by the authorities, churches were taken over, and priests were arrested. But now a more balanced situation has been reached. The churches are still not allowed to proselytize—that is, to take active steps to make converts. But believers are allowed to practice their religions, and it is even permitted to have schools where the pupils are given religious instruction—whether that religion is Orthodox, Jewish, Roman Catholic, or any other. Today there are about 9,000 Orthodox parish priests in Romania under the Patriarch Justinian.

There is perhaps a flourishing of religious activities in Romania today. Certainly all the churches are prospering. At the headquarters of the Roman Catholic Church in the Moldavian capital of Iaşi, for example, a brand-new center has been built, with a large, ornately decorated hall. But the most striking example of the present-day flourishing of religious life is the new vitality of the historic monasteries of Romania.

Back in the Middle Ages, the monasteries were the centers of Romanian culture, indeed they were the only places where culture could be said to exist. The great monasteries—Putna, Neamţ, Suceviţa, Dragomirna, Curtea de Argeş, Tismana, Horezu and many, many more—were founded by the princes of Wallachia and Moldavia over the centuries. They are all examples of a specially Romanian type of architecture, differing of course from century to century, but alike in that their builders have assimilated the styles of the Byzantine churches and monasteries in other countries, but have always added something of their own.

The church at Dragomirna, for instance, is a strangely tall, thin building, with few windows. Out of the shingled roof rises an eight-sided steeple topped by a bell-shaped cupola. Several monasteries have towers built up by a uniquely Romanian system of stone "beams" laid one on top of the other. But the supreme feature of so many of the Romanian monasteries is their frescoes—painted on the interior walls and also, in the case of the famous churches in Moldavia and Bucovina, on the outside walls as well.

Perhaps the most famous of all the painted churches is Voroneț. Every part of the outside is covered by frescoes painted in the sixteenth century in natural colors made by the peasants who lived in northern Moldavia. On the west facade is a gigantic representation of the Last Judgment: the scenes of Christ and the apostles, the blessed and the damned, are full of a sense of drama, heightened by the blood-red "river of fire" that flows down from the feet of Christ in the top center. There are also reminders of local history, with the sinners represented by obviously Turkish and Tatar personages—the deadly enemies of Stephen the Great and his successors. In another part of the fresco, there is a picture of King David playing, not his usual harp, but a tradtional Moldavian instrument, the *cobza*.

On other facades are represented a stylized vision of the Tree of

The church of the Voroneț monastery, built during the reign of Stephen the Great.

Jesse, famous for its lapis lazuli blue, scenes from the lives of saints and apostles, and an action-filled picture of the siege of Constantinople. Only on the north facade, where the rain and winds have beaten most strongly, are there signs of heavy wear and tear.

Scenes of similar power and beauty, all with their unique color effects, can be found on four other churches in the region: Sucevița, Moldovița, Humor, and Arbore. Today these churches and, in the case of Sucevița and Moldovița, of the great surrounding monasteries, too, as well as all the other great religious establishments of Romania, are being lovingly restored—at great expense—by the state. Where restorers in the past have covered over damaged wall paintings, or changed the shape of the roof to fit their own tastes, nowadays repairs are used as the occasion to rediscover the original form, with the help of contemporary documents.

But the churches, monasteries, and convents are not just tourist attractions. Nor are they merely places where the tired traveler can rest and the distracted artist find peace and quiet—though they serve these purposes. They are still above all centers of Orthodox religious life. The chanting of priests rings out from the churches at all hours of the day and night, a hammering sound echoes round the walls as a nun or priest circles the church, beating the *toaca,* a long thin piece of wood that has the same purpose as a bell.

Since the Orthodox conception of monastic life is not simply contemplative, there always appears to be a bustle of activity among the monks and nuns; some work in the fields outside the walls, providing the food for the monastery, others make religious articles: icons, crosses, vestments, and so on. Examples of the monks' labors in the past, which include some very fine works of art, are displayed in museums in the monasteries, as well as in the larger state museums around the country.

Today, however, it is not so easy to enter a monastery or nunnery as it was in the past. For anyone under fifty years old, a minimum of ten years' schooling, two in a theological school, is required. The state is anxious to ensure that the monasteries do not provide a refuge from the responsibilities of life in a socialist society.

No one can deny that the monasteries, indeed the Orthodox Church in general, has contributed a great deal to the development of Romanian art. The art of iconography is an example. Generally, Romanian icons have followed the traditional Byzantine forms and designs, but one original contribution has been the use of glass as the base. Icons painted on glass are especially, though not uniquely, associated with Transylvania. They provide an excellent illustration of the involvement of the peasant in the religious life of his village. Most of these icons have been painted by the peasants themselves, in stark colors and bold, unfussy designs. Sometimes the result is rather crude, but more often than not the icons are bright and moving expressions of religious faith and contact with nature. Icons on both glass and wood are still made by the peasants in many Romanian villages all over the country.

In times past, painting was exclusively a religious occupation. It was not until the beginning of the nineteenth century that nonreligious paintings even existed in Romania. Since then, folk art and the heritage of the church and monasteries have been the most important *Romanian* influences on the development of painting. The natural colors of the church frescoes find an echo still in many of the works you can see in Romanian galleries. The currents of western European thought were also powerful influences. In painters like Nicolae Grigorescu, Theodor Aman and, later on, Alexandru Ciucurencu and Ion Ţuculescu, you can see reflected the development of European painting as well as specially Romanian influences in choice of subject and color.

Romanian sculptors have seldom reached the same eminence as Romanian painters, but there is one remarkable exception. Constantin Brancuşi, who was born in a Romanian village in 1876 and died in Paris in 1957, was one of the world's greatest sculptors. During his long life, he developed a passion for searching for and capturing the essence of physical objects. Purity of form was his goal. And in his choice of subjects he was always influenced by memories of his childhood in Romania.

Most of Brancuşi's sculptures are now to be seen in the United States and France, but some are in Romania. In the town of Tirgu Jiu, nearly two hundred miles west of Bucharest, near his birthplace, there is a park. At the entrance stands a large gate of solid stone blocks, entitled the Gateway of the Kiss, and, at the far end, a ring of simple cylindrical "chairs" and a central stone "table," known as the Table of Silence. A short way away, at the other end of the town, is a garden in a quiet and rather dilapidated suburb, where an enormously tall column like

The Kiss. Stone sculpture by Constantin Brancuşi, 1908.

hourglasses piled one on top of the other rises up into the sky, earning this remarkable work the title of Column without End. All these are the work of Tirgu Jiu's most famous citizen, Constantin Brancusi.

In the field of music, too, some of the best-known Romanian composers, instrumentalists, and conductors (including, for example, Dinu Lipatti, the pianist, and Constantin Silvestri, the conductor) have worked a great deal outside Romania and earned international fame. Perhaps the most famous Romanian musician of all, however, the composer, violinist, pianist, conductor, and teacher, George Enescu, is also the most "Romanian" of all. That is to say, his work was interwoven with Romanian folk themes, and his strongest inspiration came from the Romanian countryside.

Every three years, in Bucharest, the George Enescu International Competition and Festival attracts some of the world's best musicians to Romania.

Today there are seventeen symphony orchestras in Romania, as well as hundreds of choirs and many other musical groups. This reflects a considerable success in popularizing music, not just folk music which has always been at the heart of Romanian life, but classical and serious modern music too. Concerts are given in quite small villages and towns, and the courses in music in schools and universities are of a high standard and are well attended.

At the same time, pop music has a large following, in spite of the fact that the authorities have always identified it with the more decadent side of life in the west—and therefore something to be viewed with great care, even suspicion. Pop music was more or less banned in Romania for many years. There is still official coolness when young singers in Romania imitate the style and the appearance of some of the wilder pop stars.

But political control is not just a feature of pop music. It applies to all branches of Romanian art and culture. In the first years of communist rule, the policy which is known as "socialist realism"—the idea that all art should make a positive contribution to the progress of the socialist state and should be readily understood by the masses—was strictly applied. Abstract painting was forbidden, and artists had to concentrate on such subjects as collective farms or factory benches. Today, the policy is applied a good deal less rigidly, but it has not been thrown out of the window. The state's opinion on what is or is not acceptable is the most important factor in an artist's life. The state is to all intents and purposes the sole buyer of art. All artists must be members of a union before they can exhibit—and union membership is subject to political control.

Censorship is more obvious in the world of literature—not only political writing, but novels, poetry, and criticism as well. The state printing and publishing organizations have a monopoly, and therefore it is impossible to have anything published in Romania without the state's approval. For all that, the atmosphere among men of letters has in recent years become more relaxed, and people are freer to write as they feel than they used to be. This in turn has meant that Romanian writers—painters and sculptors too—have had more of an impact abroad. The authorities have recognized that the restrictions on cultural life gave Romania a bad image, that of a cultural backwater, and have taken steps to see that the true value of Romanian art and artists can find expression and be appreciated in the world at large.

Literature in Romania has its origins in the Orthodox Church, just like other branches of the arts. The Orthodox Church fostered and developed printing in Romania. It was not until 1818 that the first big-scale printing press was opened in Romania; before that time the printing of books was dependent on small printing shops and the monastery workshops. But Romanian literature was late in developing, and the demand for nonreligious books was small until the nineteenth century. The oldest bookshop in Bucharest was founded by a Frenchman in 1826. The first Romanian novel was published in 1863.

Romanian intellectuals looked to German and, above all, to French culture for their stimulation. But in the last hundred years or so, a specifically Romanian literature has flourished. Many Romanian writers began to make their name, not only in Romania but also abroad; men like Eminescu, the lyric poet, Caragiale, Sadoveanu, Arghezi, Rebreanu. One of the best-known writers in recent times is Petre Dumitru, who was at one time a director of the state publishing house, but then left the country and settled in West Germany and France.

Today the publishing of books is a vast operation carried on by several state organizations. The emphasis since World War II has been on educational books, as part of the program to rid the country of illiteracy and have everyone able to read and write. It has been a huge task just to provide enough textbooks for all the new schools. The Romanian people, as a result of this program, and because books are sold at such low prices, are avid readers.

There is, too, a great demand for translation of foreign writers' works. In spite of a strict censorship on noncommunist writers from abroad (and on noncommunist writers in Romania, of course), the range and the quality of translations are impressive. Most of the major classics of world literature are readily available at bookshops all over the country; and, if they are politically acceptable, modern novels are quickly and expertly translated and distributed in many copies.

The Romanian film industry has yet to make a mark in the world. In spite of the building of some large studios near Bucharest—in 1948 there was only one studio in the country—the postwar policy of socialist realism gave the writers, actors, and directors very little scope to develop an individual style of their own. Some of the most successful films have been cartoons, which is an art form that the Romanians have mastered almost as well as the Czechoslovaks, the Poles, the Yugoslavs, and other eastern European filmmakers.

Millions of Romanians go regularly to the movies—there are 6,500 cinemas in the country. In the big towns, Bucharest especially, foreign films attract the largest audiences (in the original language or with Romanian dubbed in). French, American, British, and German film stars have, unknown to themselves, an army of enthusiastic and knowledgeable fans. Tickets are cheap because the state fixes the prices and pays the movie theaters money to make up for the small sums that they can collect from the box office.

As for the Romanian theater, it developed, as did Romanian literature as a whole, rather late. At the end of the eighteenth century and beginning of the nineteenth, the only performances that could be classed as "theater" were dramatized historical pageants and puppet shows. Slowly, there appeared more and more translations of western European classics, and highbrow literary societies read and discussed foreign plays together. Then, during the last century, several theaters were established, and some Romanian plays were written and performed.

Between the two World Wars was a great time for amateur troupes in Romania, some successful and others more or less fly-by-night. But there was also a great deal of experimentation in the major theaters of the land. Today the Romanian theater receives large subsidies from the state and, after a period in the doldrums of socialist realism, it is now a flourishing art, which attracts large and enthusiastic audiences to all of the country's forty-three theaters.

11

Customs and Folklore

Romanian folk art and folklore are some of the richest in Europe. That much is obvious to the most casual visitor. In every village there will be someone dressed in the homespun costume of the region, and on Sundays it is quite possible to see the whole population decked out in their finery.

Although the designs and the details vary from region to region, Romanian peasant costumes have many features in common: narrow white trousers and embroidered waistcoats or sheepskin jackets for men; patterned billowing blouses and heavy woven skirts (and white under-skirts) for the women. The costumes bring to mind the clothes worn by the Daco-Romans in past centuries and recall the figures depicted on Trajan's Column in Rome.

Each region in Romania is proud of its own traditional variations of dress. In the Maramureş, in the remote north of the country, for example, the men wear small ribboned straw hats, usually perched on the back of their heads. They sometimes decorate their hats with feathers, even with the tail feathers of a peacock. Women never wear hats, but caps or scarves instead.

All the costumes are made painstakingly by peasant women in their cottages. Even today, they find the time to work patiently at the long and intricate business of sewing and embroidering. The colors are never gaudy, nor the designs and patterns crude. The aim is harmony, a reflection of the harmony of the colors and patterns of nature. The same is true of Romanian rugs. The interiors of country cottages (and many town apartments, too) are full of peasant artifacts: carved furniture and utensils, pottery, cloths, and, often the most precious possession of all, rugs.

In Romanian, the rugs are called *scoarte*. This word has the same root as the French *écorce,* meaning bark (Latin *scortea*). The term in Romanian derives from the time when the interiors of the wooden peasant cottages were lined with bark to keep out the drafts. That is why the rugs are still hung on the walls rather than placed on the floor.

The rugs, made from hemp and wool, are woven now as in the past on cottage looms which are usually quite narrow, so that large rugs have to be sewn together in strips. The supreme art lies in the choice of colors and the precision of the dyeing processes, the most popular colors being traditionally black, red, green, brown, and yellow; blue was difficult to obtain as it had to come from the Orient and was expensive. The peasant women weave the rugs mainly in the fall and in winter, when their work in the fields is over.

Each pattern, peculiar to one region, has its own name, "little mouths," "sawteeth," "starlets," and so on, and the number of patterns and combinations of patterns is limitless. Oltenian rugs are famous for their flowers and animals and human figures, which mingle with the geometrical patterns. In all Romanian rug making, the influence of the Orient is very apparent. But, as in the case of architecture, the Oriental models have been adapted in a specifically Romanian way, creating a whole new tradition.

Pottery is another flourishing example of folk art, from the black pottery in northern Moldavia and northeastern Transylvania to the brown, yellow, and white plates and pots of Oltenia (notably at the monastery of Horezu) to the green and blue flower patterns on the jugs from Wallachia. The plates, dishes, and jugs from the villages are popular as ornaments in every Romanian home and are bought too by the tourists. A state organization, known as Fondul Plastic, promotes the sale of this pottery, indeed of all the traditional peasant artifacts, and its shops in all the large towns are always filled with a wide selection.

The master potters still use the traditional tools of their art, dripping the paint for the decoration onto the turning pot or plate through the tip of a cow's horn, and scooping out ornamental shapes with old-fashioned chisels. The same reverence for tradition applies to wood carving. But here there is a rivalry between the traditional methods and mass production, and the growing demands of the tourist market make it likely that the modern ways will eventually supersede the old.

One traditional folk art—though never as common as pottery or rug making and so on—was ironwork. This art goes back to Dacian times, but it flourished especially between the fifteenth and nineteenth centuries. Wrought-iron window grilles, locks and doors, candlesticks and andirons made over these years are still to be seen all over the country. Some forges still survive, such as the one attached to the monastery of Horezu.

Of course music, songs, and dancing have played a big part in the traditional life of the village, and still do. Romania boasts many musical instruments which are not to be found elsewhere: for example, the *cobza* (which features as a substitute for David's harp in the fresco at Voroneţ), the *ţambal* (cimbalom or dulcimer), the *bucium* (like an alpenhorn), and many forms of pipe or flute like the *caval* or the *cimpoi*.

The players are often Gypsies, and it is not surprising that the favorite instrument of all is the fiddle. Sometimes they accompany a girl singing a plaintive song, which sounds far more eastern than western, like the lyrical *doina,* a traditional lament which tells of love or longing. Sometimes they stand in the middle of a circle of dancers, who hop to left and right and link arms in the most famous of all Romanian dances, the *hora*.

Traditionally, joining the circle of the *hora* meant, for boys, the approach of manhood, and for girls their readiness for marriage. It used to be the custom, too, that anyone who had broken the law, or behaved in an immoral manner, was excluded from the dance; if he or she tried to join the circle the dancers immediately stopped. The basic step of the *hora* is a lilting hop on one leg and then the other, followed by sideways skips, first clockwise, then counterclockwise. It is generally performed with great verve and accompanied by whoops and yells. Sometimes it is more fun to dance than to watch, if the caustic commènt of an eighteenth-century French traveler is anything to go by. He compared the dancers to the performing bears that the Gypsies would take on exhibition round the countryside and remarked, "I have always wondered if it is the Moldavians who taught the bears to dance or the bears who taught the Moldavians!"

But our traveler must have witnessed a particularly clumsy performance. The villagers are usually expert dancers, and perform a large number of dances, like the *sirba* (the "Serbian dance," which in Serbia is called the "Wallachian dance"!) or the *briul*. Basically, there are nine or ten types of Romanian folk dances, but thousands of local variations.

In times past, young men would become the so-called "devil's dancers." This meant that for three, five, or seven years (it had to be an odd number, or else the pact was not binding) they would make an undertaking with the devil to dance at every moment of their waking hours. In return they would be given food and drink, and the devil would make them irresistible to the village girls. Whenever a group of young devil's dancers arrived in a village they would be feted immediately and the wild celebrations would begin.

One of the most difficult of all the dances is the *caluşari*. It used to have much more of a ritual significance than it has today. Before

A peasant dance in Moldavia.

Whitsun, nine young men belonging to nine neighboring villages, decked out in embroidered waistcoats and ribboned hats, wearing spurs and bells on their boots, would dance for hours on end. Oaths were taken against evil spirits and the dancers carried sticks and other symbolic objects such as a piece of hareskin, and a pole decorated with garlic. Sick people were said to be cured if the dancers leaped over them. Today, much of the mysterious ritual has disappeared. But the dance itself remains popular, and, performed by amateur folk-dance troupes, it has won Romania many international competitions.

The ritual of the *caluşari* at Whitsun is one among many rituals and customs associated with different seasons or religious festivals. Around Christmas and the New Year, miming plays are performed, hymns and songs are sung and, as in so many countries, the fir tree is decorated. On New Year's Eve, the children go from house to house singing *colinde,* tradtional carols and songs to bring luck and prosperity. At the same time the *capra* or goat dance is performed and dancing goes on around the *plugușor,* or little plow, and the children wave bunches of paper flowers, all of which is said to bring good fortune.

In spring the shepherds' celebrations come to the fore as this is the time when the flocks are driven up into the mountains and the shepherds have in front of them long months of minding the sheep and living in isolated huts miles from the villages. The *Ariet* is a celebration in honor of this annual event, and it is accompanied by singing and dancing and a great deal of eating and drinking.

On midsummer's day, there are special dances and songs, which vary from region to region. In Transylvania, for instance, young girls go out into the fields, weave together wild flowers and throw them over the cottages to bring luck to the people in the village. Harvest festival has its own ceremonies too, although the church is nowadays less associated with them.

The same is true of the marriage ceremonies, now that the state is officially atheistic. But many of the traditional customs still survive, the processions, the songs, the carrying of the fir tree from the bridegroom's house to the bride's, the pretended resistance put up by the bride's family when the bridegroom comes to collect her, the reciting of traditional poems.

When there is death in the village, the old customs of the wake and the burial are still carried on. The great funeral songs of northern Oltenia, southwest Transylvania, and the Banat—*zorile* (the dawns), *bradul* (the fir tree), and *cintecul cel mare* (the great song)—are sung by the mourners; there are traditional dirges and masks.

Romanian folklore is rich in epic songs, recalling the days of resistance to the Turks and Tatars, and telling of the centuries of suffering of the peasants, or of great dramas of love and friendship. There are traditional shepherds' ballads, too; the most famous is the story of *Miorița,* the ewe lamb. One of the greatest stories told, or sung in traditional ballads, is that of Manole, the master builder. Variations of it exist throughout the Balkans.

It is the story of fidelity to a vow. *Meșterul* Manole is building the monastery of Argeș on the orders of an ambitious *voevod* (prince). One night the walls collapse and, according to superstition, someone has to be sealed into the new walls. They draw lots to find who shall be sacrificed. Manole vows he will obey the laws of chance. By means of trickery, his fellow builders arrange the lot to fall on his wife, although she is absent and is unaware of her fate. The master builder cannot escape the consequences of his vow. So great is his love for his wife that nature itself tries to prevent her from approaching the church. But she fights her way through the storms and other obstacles. She loves her husband so much that she agrees to put herself in the wall for him, although at first she cannot quite believe that he is serious. She sings a final song of parting as Manole and the builders feverishly pile up the bricks around her. The master builder's only satisfaction is that he constructs the finest church in all Romania. In one version of the ballad, Manole condemns himself to a lifetime of erecting more and more beautiful walls, impoverishing his family in the process.

Romanian folklore is lovingly studied and preserved by special institutes and by academicians. It is regarded as an important part of Romanian literature and history. Its richness attracts many foreign folklorists.

In a similar way, the state preserves and studies old Romanian buildings, not just churches, monasteries, and palaces, but ordinary peasant homes. In Bucharest there is one of the finest museums of peasant houses in the world. It contains examples of houses from every region of the country literally transported from the depths of the countryside to the site in a park on the north side of the capital. This *Museul Satului*—the "Village Museum"—is a center of attraction for thousands of visitors, Romanian and foreign, every year. It contains not only the houses themselves but their entire interiors, decorations, utensils, and furniture. Outside, in the barns, you can see many of the simple implements used to till the land and carry the crops. The museum was projected just before World War II, but it was developed under the present government.

In a country with such a violent past as Romania, where Dracula was a reality, and a peasant's life was rough, brutish, and short, it was natural that superstition should flourish. Like superstitions everywhere, most relate to bad luck—what brings it and how to avoid it. In Romania it is bad luck to set out on a journey on a Tuesday, and on Saturday it is said that there are always three hours during the day when things go wrong. Dreaming of a young child, especially of bathing a young child, brings bad luck, and so does an owl if it sits on your roof at night and hoots—that could even signal a death in the family.

When you leave your house in the morning, you must remember to put your right foot outside first, and, if you remember something you have left behind, don't go back to get it; that will bring you bad luck all day. As you set off down the road, beware that you don't cross the path of a priest; priests may be respected figures, but if you meet one first thing in the morning, that will mean a bad day for you!

Knocking on wood, just as in America, is one usual way to ward off bad luck, but there are other ways too, such as crossing oneself beneath a full moon.

Superstitions survive, naturally enough, more in the villages than in the towns, since most of them have their origins in the struggle between the peasant and an apparently hostile nature. But even in the countryside superstitious fears have far less force than they used to. The legendary horrors of Dracula, which up until quite recent times could spread terror through whole communities if there were rumors of his return, are now laughed at by the science-conscious children in the village schools.

But traditional proverbs reflecting centuries of accumulated wisdom and wit are still a part of everyday speech—again in the villages more than the towns. Romania is as rich in them as any eastern European country. Many of the proverbs reflect the injustices to which the peasants were subjected: "Justice is as the rulers make it," runs one saying, and "The man who goes to law often loses an ox to win a cat," another. The sensible way to resist, according to the Romanian peasant, is summed up in the proverb: "If a dog barks at you, stop his muzzle with bread"; and there is a similar one: "Kiss the hand you cannot bite."

The poverty of the peasants contrasted with the riches of the boyars gave rise to many sayings. The peasants complained that riches allowed the strangest tastes to be satisfied: "With money one can even buy rabbit cheese"! The traditional attitude to the backbreaking work in the fields is expressed in the proverb: "May God grant holidays all the year round, and only one working day, and then let that be a wedding."

The caution of the Romanians is expressed in such proverbs as: "If you cannot catch anything, don't stretch out your hand"; another favorite is: "It's easier to inherit than to earn."

The hard life of the country and the toughness of the peasant is summed up in the saying: "May God never give the Romanian as much as he can bear."

12

The Land and the People Today

The floods of the early summer of 1970 almost drowned the entire country. The rains fell on the hills and on the plains, and huge volumes of snow in the Carpathians began to melt. The water flowed down into already swollen rivers, and all this water, leaving behind a trail of broken houses, mud, and debris, flowed into the Danube, causing even more flooding. Hundreds of thousands of people were made homeless, many died. Even criminals were released from their prisons to help build dykes and protect farms and factories and homes.

The floods of 1970 were a disaster not only because of the unfortunate people who suffered. They were also a disaster because they held up the fast progress that Romania was making. We have seen how long it took Romania to develop from the dark ages and form a civilized society; and how so often in history the Romanian lands suffered from the clashes between the bigger European powers. It is only for a hundred years or less that Romania can properly be called a modern state. World War II had terrible consequences for Romania— as bad as any war during her history. But the country slowly recovered in the following years, and is on the verge of a new prosperity. The floods have not destroyed all the fruits of this progress, but they did show how dangerous a natural disaster can be to a country like Romania.

The aftermath of the 1970 floods.

Romania is still basically a land of peasants—like other countries in eastern Europe. The peasants, working now for the most part on collective farms, depend on good harvests for their livelihood. Over the years, many have left the land and gone to live in the towns, but millions have stayed in the Romanian countryside, living according to traditions that have been handed down over the centuries.

The collective farms—or cooperatives—are run along the lines first established in Soviet Russia in the 1930s. The land is owned by all the peasants in a particular area, and the profits, after the state has claimed its share of the crops, are divided up according to the number of days each man or woman has worked. Some of the wages are paid in kind, that is to say by handing over to the peasants a part of the farm produce. There are also very large state farms in Romania, where the land itself is owned by the state and wages are paid just as if the peasants were factory workers in the towns. Peasant families are still allowed to keep a small plot of land for themselves, on which they can keep a cow, or one or two smaller animals, and grow a small amount of crops. The traditional plum brandy, *ţuica,* is made still in some country cottages, but nowadays the state has taken over almost entirely from the peasants and makes the brandy on a large scale.

In some parts of Romania, where there are mountains and forests, the land has never been collectivized, because it is impossible to make large farms in this difficult terrain. The peasants here cultivate the land very much as they have done for centuries, although today they are better off, as the lines from electricity grids reach into their cottages, and the state's social security offers them help when they are ill or in difficulties. But the twentieth century is only just reaching into the remoter corners of the country, and the 1970 floods held up even this slow progress.

In the towns, the changes from the past are much more obvious. Great apartment buildings, new hotels—such as the Intercontinental in the center of Bucharest—rise high above the low skylines. There are

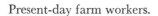

Present-day farm workers.

supermarkets in the main streets, and giant factories in the suburbs. Most of the one- or two-man workshops, the ateliers, where shoes were mended, or wood polished, or any number of other tasks performed, have now disappeared.

One thing that is different about Romanian towns, when compared with towns in the United States of America, is that there is very little advertising—hardly any colored lights, billboards, or flashing signs. This means that the cities appear to western eyes at first glance colorless; but there is the advantage that the buildings can be seen better and the cities appear less cluttered.

There are also far fewer automobiles per person in Romania than in the United States. The Romanians are making their own automobiles now, modeled on a Renault design from France, but there is hardly any traffic congestion yet. The accident rate, however, is very high. In the countryside there are as many oxcarts and buffalo carts as automobiles and trucks. Much of the plowing of the land is still done by horses, or by oxen, although tractors are being used more and more.

Because everything made in Romania is produced in state-run factories, there is seldom a great variety of goods in the shops. A state council decides how much of any one thing is to be produced, and where; and the factory has merely to obey its instructions. When state control was tightest in Romania, especially in the 1950s, the planning officials took very little notice of what the people wanted. They decided everything themselves. Now the people who buy in the shops have more choice, and the factories take more notice of their tastes. But Romania is still far from a market economy where the consumer is the master.

Food comes into the big towns from the collective farms and the state farms in the country, but there are also markets in many places to which the peasants can bring their own fruit and vegetables. They set them out on stalls early in the morning and remain throughout the day, shouting their wares and chatting and gossiping among themselves. When there are shortages in the market, President Ceaușescu has been

A Dacia 1300 on the assembly line.

known to make unexpected visits to see what is happening and why there are not enough goods.

Generally speaking, the peasants seldom leave their native villages except to come to the local town. But many Romanians travel all over the country for their holidays (few obtain passports as yet for holidaying abroad). They know their country well, in all its variety: the mountains, with their ski resorts and climbing routes; the seaside, where famous international resorts like Mamaia rise out of the miles of golden sands along the Black Sea coast; and the rolling valleys of Moldavia, where the ancient monasteries stand, calm and serene beside the forest-covered slopes. They know too the fortified castles of Transylvania, the wooden churches of the Maramureş, in the remote north of the country: and the long flat stretches of the Danube with its delta that harbors hundreds of varieties of birds, fishes, and animals. All these delights for vacationers are now also becoming known to people from other lands, as tourists flock into the country—a country which for many years hardly saw a visitor from "outside."

A favorite Romanian occupation is a cure at one of the many health spas in the country. At Eforie, on the Black Sea coast, for example, thousands of people undress and coat themselves with the mud from the shores of the inland lake there. This, it is claimed, helps the bones and the muscles, calms the nerves, and eases the breathing—in fact, cures just about any ailment you like. It must be effective, because Eforie, as well as many other mudbath spas, is always teeming with black, naked bodies. Every year, at the state's expense, not far short of a million people visit these mud baths and the spas where the waters are warm and contain health-giving minerals.

New roads crisscross Romania today, many of them spectacular, built through or along the edge of the mountains, such as the road through the craggy rocks of the Bicaz gorge. There are scenic routes along the valleys of many rivers, like the Olt and the Prahova. New roads lead now to the Danube delta, too. But in most country areas, there are still only rough tracks.

The railroad system was started many years ago in Romania (though not without many financial scandals, as we saw earlier). Today a network of tracks covers the country. The Orient Express and the Wiener Walzer, two great transcontinental expresses, link Bucharest with western Europe. But you must be careful when booking tickets on a Romanian train. Remember to buy one ticket for the train itself, one more for a seat, and yet another if the train is a *rapid,* or express!

Traveling inside Romania is cheap, whether by train, plane, bus, or automobile. So too are such things as the telephone, and power from electricity, and natural gas. Nevertheless, Romanian people earn a good deal less than people doing the same job in the west, so the prices do not appear quite so low to them.

Inevitably there are many daily frustrations when living in a "bureaucratic" state. Shopping, for example, is not made easy. When buying food in a supermarket, you have first to inspect the goods and choose what you want, then line up for a ticket, and finally line up once again to collect what you have bought. As shops are almost always crowded, the lines can sometimes be very long.

When tired and thirsty after shopping or after a long day's work—office work begins at seven in the morning and carries on to about three thirty without a break—there are always the restaurants and cafés to go to. In Bucharest, and other cities too, there are extensive parks and, in the summer, the open-air restaurants, known as "summer gardens," come into their own. Beside each table stands a bucket of ice on a sort of metal tripod; bottles of beer, mineral water, and Pepsi-Cola (made under license in Romania) lie in them, needing only to be opened by a passing waiter. Open-air restaurants surround the great lakes and canals which cover the northern part of Bucharest; they are favorite meeting places on hot summer evenings, when Gypsy musicians play their violins and sing their plaintive songs.

Another popular recreation in Romania is sports. Soccer matches

The modern center of Bucharest. Congress Hall is on the left.

attract enormous crowds every Sunday, and millions also play soccer in clubs and schools and so on. Participation in sports of all kinds is actively encouraged by the authorities, who have provided the funds for an enormous expansion in the number of sporting facilities up and down the country. There are huge notices at stadiums and such places urging the population to take more exercise and play games for their health. Popular sports are basketball and volleyball, boxing, swimming, rock-climbing, cycling, and skiing: rugby football and tennis attract more players and supporters every day. But it's still soccer that beats all the others. On big soccer occasions, such as the World Cup, or a key championship match, the streets will empty as the entire population, or so it appears, shouts for the teams in the stadium or watches more peacefully in front of the television.

There are, too, thousands of enthusiasts for all kinds of amateur hobbies, from model making to ham radio operating, stamp collecting, and chess. Romanians have a reputation for their mechanical inventiveness, and their success in international competitions bears this out.

Radio and television, when they are not being used as the means to put out the Party's propaganda, provide a popular entertainment service. A large amount of time on the air is devoted to the promotion of Romanian culture, and both radio and television, as in most other countries, are serving more and more as education media.

Science and foreign language programs are followed assiduously by millions. The most popular language of all is English. It is the first choice of language, too, in schools and universities. In the past, French was a natural choice for the well-educated classes: there was a strong cultural link with France, and the languages share the same Latin root —both being so-called "romance" languages. Then, for some years after World War II, when the Russian influence was strongest, all schoolchildren had to learn Russian. Now there is a free choice for all students of modern languages. No doubt many children decide to learn English so that they can follow the words of their favorite pop songs and pronounce the names of singers and groups that they have heard and have read about! But they are well aware that English will be useful to them later, too, in whatever career they decide to follow.

Before World War II there were far fewer schools than there are now in Romania. Today, schooling is compulsory for eight years, and most schoolchildren carry on their studies for longer. They are encouraged especially to become skilled in scientific and technical subjects, for the country has a great need of scientists, engineers, doctors, dentists, and so on. Such people were rare before the war, when law and the arts were more popular subjects.

Already the number of doctors and engineers per person of the population in Romania is one of the highest in the world. As far as possible, every little village or group of villages has its own doctor. Sometimes they are only trained for basic repairs and for preventive medicine, but at least the country people have someone to go to when they are ill or break a bone. The average age of the people has there-

A high school class.

fore risen steeply in the last quarter of a century.

Similar progress has been made in the field of education: before World War II, millions of Romanians could not read or write. Now it is claimed that everybody can master these basic skills, and, although that is certainly an exaggeration, years of compulsory education and the building of more schools and the training of more teachers have indeed all contributed to a rapid rate of progress.

So Romania is slowly overcoming the disadvantages which geography and history have imposed upon her. No one can say that the years of communist rule have been wholly beneficial, or that the material improvements of the last few years would not have come (to a greater or lesser extent) whatever political system was in operation. But the unanswerable logic of events has given Romania a communist government and, at least as long as Soviet Russia is also ruled by a communist government, it is difficult to see any major change coming to Romania. Not even those who are against the communist system would all argue that the complete abolition of socialism is now desirable, since it could cause disruption and perhaps civil strife, and has proved its value in many fields.

Generally speaking the past (as represented by the monasteries and churches, peasant customs and folklore, intellectual and artistic traditions) has learned to coexist peacefully enough with the present (as represented by collectivization, industralization, and Party control over individual freedom). There are of course still problems, the greatest of which is to make the socialist system work efficiently and humanely. But the Romanian people have learned through hard experience how to live with problems. Sometimes, as for instance during the Soviet invasion of Czechoslovakia in 1968, or during the terrible floods of 1970, Romanians feel that the nation is fragile and ignored by the rest of the world. But the inner resistance of the Romanian people is strong. Their very survival through a long and turbulent history is sufficient proof.

Index

About the Author

Julian Hale was born and spent most of his life in the British Isles. He studied at Christ Church, Oxford, and subsequently at the Institut Universitaire des Hautes Etudes Internationales in Geneva. He has worked with the United Nations Economic Commission for Europe, and has been a program planner for the BBC's Romanian Service since 1969. Mr. Hale has traveled extensively, speaks six languages—including Romanian —and has written another book, *Ceausescu's Romania,* for adults. He is married to American writer Mary Kathleen Benet.